The Breakaway

Bryan Smith

The Inside Story of

the Wirtz Family Business

and the Chicago Blackhawks

Foreword by Tony Esposito

Northwestern University Press
Evanston, Illinois

Northwestern University Press
www.nupress.northwestern.edu

Photographs courtesy of Rocky Wirtz.

A portion of the royalties from this book will benefit the Chicago Blackhawks Foundation.

Printed in the United States of America

10 9 8 7 6 5 4 3 2

ISBN 978-0-8101-3888-9 (cloth)
ISBN 978-0-8101-3889-6 (ebook)

Cataloging-in-Publication data are available from the Library of Congress.

For Leah and my mother, Jo

Breakaway (noun):

1. *Ice hockey.* A sudden rush down the ice by a [hockey] player or players in an attempt to score a goal, after breaking clear of defending opponents.

2. An act or instance of breaking away; secession; separation.

3. A person or thing that breaks away.

—Dictionary.com

Contents

Foreword

Tony Esposito

In the spring of 1972, after our season ended, my wife Marilyn and I had a dinner at our home in Elmhurst. Pat and Jackie Stapleton were there. So were Bobby and Joanne Hull. Besides getting together for a few laughs, our mission that night was to convince Bobby to stay with the Blackhawks. He was being heavily recruited by the Winnipeg Jets of a proposed new league, the World Hockey Association.

"It will all work out here, Bobby."

That's what we kept telling him, but it didn't register. Later that evening, Bobby picked up the phone and called Ben Hatskin, the owner of the Jets, to tell him, "I'm coming!"

In June, Bobby left for the WHA. It was a decision heard around the sports world and nowhere louder than in Chicago.

Everybody was shocked. It bothered a lot of people. We went to the Stanley Cup finals the next year, but we didn't have the "hammer" like Bobby who could break a game open. We lost, and pretty soon, the window on our team closed. We had a great team, but we never won the Cup.

My journey with the Blackhawks began in 1969. When I joined the team, the Wirtz family had owned it since rescuing the franchise in the 1950s. Had it not been for the Wirtz family's willingness to invest in the Blackhawks, they might have moved and left Chicago without a team in the National Hockey League. At one point, the Blackhawks actually staged "home" games in neutral cites such as Minneapolis, Omaha, Indianapolis, and St. Louis—hard to believe considering the team's popularity now.

It was a different time. Marilyn and I socialized with Arthur Wirtz and Virginia, his very elegant wife, as well as Arthur's son Bill and his wife, Joan. They were all classy people, and our relationships were respectful and genuine. The Wirtzes were always accessible and willing to help.

When Arthur passed away in 1983, Bill took over and the connection between ownership and players continued. Bill and Joan were fun to be around. He was a great storyteller who could go the distance with players less than half his age. We had a lot of late nights that would go into early mornings. It was special, as was the way I negotiated my contracts—never through the team's general manager or my agent, but directly with Bill. He treated my family and me well, very well.

Bill was also incredibly generous with charitable causes, but in a private way. I know a lot of that had to do with Joan, who kept him in his lane and kept him grounded. For many years, Bill also served as chairman of the NHL Board of Governors, fighting hard for his team and the sport. Through it all, he was always approachable.

Once, I asked him why he didn't put home games on television, and he responded tersely, "because fans won't come to the building if they can watch the team at home." I never revisited that issue with him, and it was an issue that remained until his death in 2007.

All professional sports teams go through cycles. It's part of the business. In the 1950s, the Blackhawks were in critical condition until the Wirtzes saved them. The Blackhawks won the Stanley Cup in 1961, their first since 1938, and were contenders for most of the decade. We fared well during the early '70s, then felt the loss of Bobby, and revived during the '80s. But as years went on, the league expanded, new teams marketed the sport, and not televising home games loomed larger, as did Bill's defiance.

In the 1990s, the Blackhawks really started going south. Good players left, often in a negative way. Doug Wilson, Steve Larmer, Ed Belfour, and Jeremy Roenick moved to other teams and played well. Also, Chris Chelios, a Chicago native, asked to be traded to a team dedicated to winning—a commitment he did not feel from the Blackhawks' management.

For me and many of my former teammates, it was painful to watch the downward spiral of a proud franchise. It was an era marked by dramatic roster turnovers, frequent coaching changes, and fan anger or, what's worse, fan apathy. The Blackhawks were slowly slipping into irrelevance—home crowds were sparse, sponsors fleeing, and even Chicago newspapers stopped covering the team on the road. The atmosphere throughout the franchise was hostile.

It's difficult to pinpoint what caused the demise. Some speculated that Bill was never the same after Joan passed away in 1983, the same year Arthur died. She was a strong figure in his life and the mother of their five children. Others suggest that the franchise lost its way after Bill suffered several debilitating strokes. Perhaps it was a combination of those things. Regardless, Bill never let go of the steering wheel, nor did anyone seize it, despite his failing health and some less-than-rational decisions.

Shortly before Bill passed away, he rued that the Blackhawks had lost close to two hundred million in recent years. From my front office experience with the Pittsburgh Penguins and Tampa Bay Lightning, I can tell you that statement floored me. He was using money from his other companies to fund a hockey team that was in serious trouble.

When Bill died, many of us mourned from a distance. I can't speak for others, but for Marilyn and me, it wasn't anger that kept us from attending the funeral service. It was a feeling that we just wouldn't be welcome. I was told there were not many former players there. Still, I never lost respect for Bill. The man I knew was compassionate, honorable, and in his better days, a true asset to hockey. Unfortunately, the perception of Bill among fans and the media was the complete opposite.

Most of us assumed that Rocky Wirtz would take over the Wirtz Corporation while his younger brother, Peter, would continue to run the Blackhawks as he had done under his father for years. I knew Peter, but I didn't know Rocky that well. Whenever I checked in, Rocky was overseeing the family's liquor wholesale business and, by all accounts, doing it very well.

As a player, I would see Rocky at some team events, but he was never really in the mix. He showed up for the Christmas party and team picture and that was about it. I remember talking to him, and at times, he just didn't seem comfortable. Peter, meanwhile, was a day-to-day fixture with the team. We were curious about what role, if any, Rocky might have with the Blackhawks.

The answer came just a few days after Bill's funeral. Peter abruptly stepped away, requiring Rocky to assume control immediately. I, along with many others, believe the legacy of the Blackhawks changed forever at that moment.

Rocky could have eased his way into the situation, but the fact is he couldn't afford to wait to fix the Blackhawks. They were hemorrhaging money and had become virtually invisible. He had to allocate funds to cover payroll and expenses. He had to make dramatic moves in the front office. And he had to act fast.

Among the first of numerous smart decisions by Rocky was to have lunch with John McDonough, a decorated executive with the Chicago Cubs. Rocky was certain John was the man to run the Blackhawks. John accepted Rocky's offer and, almost immediately, you could sense a seismic shift in the organization.

Rocky and John made it clear from day one: the goal is to win the Stanley Cup. There would be no division among departments, no agendas. Nothing short of a group effort would be acceptable. John also stressed that the Blackhawks were out of the "grudge business."

Suddenly, the organization functioned as a unit. Ownership, management, coaches, players, employees, interns were on the same page—and treated accordingly. The fact that everyone, from players to the front office staff to ambassadors like me, received the same championship rings after the Blackhawks won the Stanley Cup in 2010, 2013, and 2015—is testament to the new culture.

When I retired in 1984, I never imagined I would be back with the Blackhawks. But Rocky and John have brought Bobby, Stan Mikita, Denis Savard, and me back into the family. I never envisioned other former Blackhawks who didn't leave on good terms being embraced. Or visiting former Blackhawks who are now playing for other teams being saluted on the United Center video board. I never foresaw the arena being a sea of red sweaters, and sellouts every game.

It has been a remarkable experience for me, and I know I am not alone. Bobby says the call from the Blackhawks changed his life. Stan said he waited thirty years for the phone to ring. We have not only been welcomed back, we've been welcomed home.

What would have happened to the Blackhawks had these amazing changes not occurred? Would they have won the three Stanley Cups in six years despite a hard salary cap? Would there have been the "greatest sports-business turnaround ever" as chronicled by *Forbes* magazine? Would the Wirtz family have spent $75 million to build a state-of-the-art ice arena, not just as a practice facility for the Blackhawks, but as a place where Chicago's children and at-risk youth can learn about hockey and life's lessons?

I confess that when I first heard about Rocky's plan to commit those resources, I questioned his reasoning. He pursued his vision, and today that vision is a state-of-the-art building teeming with kids on skates. I was wrong, and I am happy about it.

When I was asked to write this foreword for the *The Breakaway*, I was asked to do so through the lens of my hockey career. What follows in the book is from a different vantage point, perhaps a tougher one. But the sport and the business of hockey are tough, as are the people within it.

I am honored to be even a small part of *The Breakaway*. I will always be grateful for my days as a player with the Chicago Blackhawks and I am excited about my current role as team ambassador. Last but not least, I am proud that proceeds from *The Breakaway* will benefit the Chicago Blackhawks Foundation and the incredible work it does for our communities and our children.

Tony Esposito joined the Blackhawks as a rookie goalie in 1969 and recorded fifteen shutouts, a single-season club record unlikely to be broken. He was inducted into the Hockey Hall of Fame in 1988; in the same year, his number 35 was retired by the Blackhawks. For the National Hockey League's centennial celebration in 2017, Esposito was voted one of the hundred greatest players ever.

The Breakaway

Prologue
A Good Burger

The kid, maybe twelve, maybe thirteen, shied up in his Blackhawks sweater, the big, red home jersey with the black and white stripes and the Indian head with the inscrutable smile.

Cap pulled low, jeans bagging around a pair of scuffed Air Jordans, he stood on the cusp of the concourse, uncertain in the churning swirl of lights and sound and loose clusters of laughing, rosy-faced men whether to go through with it. His self-consciousness flared under the gaze of a pair of ushers in dark blazers with the words United Center Security *stitched in white.*

The kid was thin, not quite gangly, with shy, polite eyes, and a ball of blond fuzz peeking out from under his cap. He was dressed almost identically to thousands of others in the packed stadium, yet he felt marked. A reassuring glance from his father, who followed behind, nudged him forward and he stepped fully onto the concourse.

He had worked up the nerve to speak to a man who sat a few feet away on one of about twenty folding chairs arranged to match the curve of the concourse floor. In a gray suit with a light-blue tie, the man certainly didn't seem intimidating. He was smiling and laughing, shaking hands, occasionally leaning over to say something to a man next to him, who happened to be the commissioner of the league.

The kid watched it all and then found himself caught up in the flashing, pulsing swirl around him. The arena, vast and bright, yawned like an immense vault. Stretched across the top, a long line of banners, including three Stanley Cup championship standards, hung overhead. The scoreboard, big as a rocket booster, flashed a series of videos: the old legend, Bobby Hull, skidding to a stop in a cloud of glittering ice spray, blades biting ice as he fired a rifle shot over the glove hand of a twisting goalie; Patrick Kane, slipping the puck between the pads of a sprawled netminder for a championship winner; the faces, one by one, of the current team, their expressions as menacing as the Metallica song thundering through the arena.

And far below, the ice. First blue, then red, then white under laser lights, the surface shimmered like cake frosting. Players wove and slashed, blasting hard shots off the boards, one puck soaring into the stands.

The kid, at last, made his move.

At his age, he had no way of knowing how astonishing it was that the owner of his favorite team, the Chicago Blackhawks, was perched right there, on a folding chair, among the anonymous thousands—not like his predecessor, sitting in his private club, tinkling the ice in his drink and grousing over his pitiful team. The kid had no way of knowing the suffering the thousands around him had endured before the man he wanted to talk to had taken over—the long, dark, agonizing decades when most people would rather have dumped a beer on the owner's head than approach him for a few words and a selfie. Certainly the boy couldn't know how much it cost the man personally: the scorn of his brother, the fury of their father; the dark machinations of that father to keep him—his own son—from taking over.

The boy couldn't know and didn't. But no matter. When he approached at last, he said what he had come to say. "I saw you had the burger. I had it too."

The man twisted in his folding chair. "Pardon?" he said.

"The burger. My dad and I were in the same restaurant as you earlier downstairs. I saw you had the burger. I had it too."

"You're right," the owner said with a smile. "Did you like it?"

"Yes." The kid then looked from the man back to his dad standing behind him. "I also wanted to say thank you," he said, "for putting the home games on TV."

At this, William Rockwell Wirtz broke into a surprised grin and, glancing from son to father, said, "You're very welcome."

The boy grinned and looked at his dad, who said, "Thank you, Mr. Wirtz."

"You're welcome. Call me Rocky."

A Legacy of Boos

He knew it was coming, could feel it like the menace of a looming storm. *This night. On top of everything else. Dad's death. The empire tottering. The team, the crown jewel of that empire, limping into the new season, millions in the hole before the first puck was dropped. The family name, once an emblem of esteem, admiration, dignity to the city, to the world—now the subject of derision, taunts, mockery.*

And now this. Everyone knows how the fans felt about him. Surely they know what's about to happen . . .

William Rockwell Wirtz—"Rocky"—shifted uncomfortably in the cool luxury of the owner's suite at the United Center in Chicago's West Loop, a skybox aerie of leather seats, recessed lighting, and glistening bottles of top-shelf spirits laid in by the family's vast liquor, wine, and wholesale concern. Rocky's four siblings, their faces reflecting varying degrees of apprehension and anguish, ambled about him in the muddled haze of the freshly bereaved.

At fifty-five, Rocky was a squarely built man whose features and bone structure marked him as a Wirtz as surely as the engraved nameplate that guarded the entrance to his office. He had a somewhat low shelf of brow divided by two deep creases, a square jaw scaffolding a mouth bracketed on either side by equally deep furrows, and a broom-brush thick head of medium-brown hair, parted left to right. Rocky liked to smile and occasionally flashed a slightly mischievous grin, the prelude to a sotto voce zinger, usually a quip, but sometimes, too, a cutting remark that sliced as precisely as a surgeon's scalpel.

Similar features could be found on the taller, leaner figure standing not far from Rocky—Peter Wirtz, Rocky's younger brother by seven years. As the clock ticked down to the start of the ceremony Peter had arranged—nay, insisted upon—he wore a stoic expression reflective of the almost paralyzing grief he was feeling, hardened by his determination to see this moment through.

It was just after 6:30 P.M. on Saturday, October 6, 2007, the Blackhawks' home opener, and the arena already thrummed with the arrival of a large crowd. Ordinarily, Rocky would have forgone the posh comforts of the owner's skybox, opting instead to take up his usual seat on a folding chair among the fans just inside the entrance to section 119. But this was no ordinary night—and, if what he feared came to pass, it would be no ordinary opening-night ceremony.

Eleven days earlier, Rocky's father, Bill, the controversial and reviled president of the Blackhawks, had died following a short bout with cancer. The loss reverberated not just in Chicago, but virtually anywhere in the world that cherished professional hockey. Bill Wirtz, like him or not, had dominated the league.

Big and barrel chested, with a fleshy, pitted nose, flashing dark eyes, and a rosacea-blotched face twisted into what seemed a perpetual scowl, Bill had boasted eighteen years of iron-fisted rule as chairman of the National Hockey League's Board of Governors and forty-one years as president of one of its crown-jewel franchises. In the early decades of his reign, he had built the team into a perennial winner and Stanley Cup contender whose achievements included a streak of twenty-eight straight playoff appearances. As chairman of the vast Wirtz empire built by his father, Bill had burnished his reputation as a businessman by expanding the company's sprawling portfolio of real estate, banking interests, and liquor wholesaling.

Mercifully for the family, much of the early news coverage of Bill's death focused on those accomplishments, along with his many private acts of kindness and generosity. Denis Savard, a Hall of Famer who spent ten seasons with the Blackhawks and was head coach at the time of Bill's death, recalled turning to the president as a nineteen-year-old desperate to help his family. "I called [him] up, and said, 'I need $10,000,'" Savard told the suburban Chicago *Daily Herald*. "'You can take it off my check.' Guess what? He never took it off."

Hawks general manager Dale Tallon recalled that when his own father was given six months to live, Wirtz "told me and my family not to worry." He said "he'd take care of things—and he did." When Keith Magnuson, the beloved defenseman-turned-ambassador to the Blackhawks, was killed in a car accident, Bill Wirtz footed the bill for expenses.

At the crowded funeral service at the Fourth Presbyterian Church on Chicago's Michigan Avenue, former NHL Commissioner John Ziegler began by addressing the deceased. "Bill, you've got a full house," he said with a smile. Then he turned serious. "He loved the Blackhawks. He loved the NHL, he loved the game of hockey," Ziegler said. "But he had a greater love and that was the Wirtz family."

It was a bittersweet statement for Rocky, whom his father had shunned in the last years of his life, and whose own children—Bill's grandkids—had received letters from their grandfather telling them not to bother to show up for Thanksgiving dinner. "Don't worry," he added, according to Rocky. "I'll drop your Christmas presents off."

For many of the fans, nothing, not even death, could mask the scorn and fury they felt toward Bill Wirtz, who had turned their team—one of the so-called Original Six of the NHL—from powerhouse to laughingstock, a judgment all but enshrined in 2004 when ESPN named the Blackhawks the worst franchise not just in hockey, but in all of pro sports.

More infuriatingly, Bill had done so with a sort of perverse delight, a defiance that jabbed a thumb in the eye of the generations of fans who had sunk heart and soul into the fortunes of the team. First and most famously, he had refused to televise regular-season home games, assuming that it would undermine attendance, and he had clung to that decision with an obstinacy that in the final years of his life seemed based as much on spite as any deeply held principle. He simply could not—or would not—admit he had been wrong. He had alienated past Hawks legends, including the most iconic of them all, the "Golden Jet," Bobby Hull. He had fired one of the team's most successful coaches, the colorful and beloved Billy Reay, by having a card slipped under Reay's door a few days before Christmas. And year after year he had lowballed salaries for players and coaches to the point that *Chicago Tribune* columnist Bob Verdi tagged him with a moniker that would follow him to his grave: Dollar Bill.

By the late 1990s, relations with fans had corroded so completely that on the few occasions when Bill ventured into the public eye—as when he presented Savard with his retired number 18 jersey during a pregame ceremony at the new United Center in 1998—the crowd drowned his remarks with boos loud enough to shake the rafters. He responded to such humiliations not with apologies or even anger but taunts. "They're getting weak," he said of the fans after the Savard debacle. "They were much louder in the old building."

Rocky fully understood the situation, which is why he worried about the agenda for this night. Over his strenuous objections, Peter had arranged a ceremony to honor Bill, climaxed by a moment of silence. The idea—incredibly, in Rocky's opinion—was endorsed by his other siblings, including sisters Gail, Karey, and Alison. To Rocky, the notion felt like dangling a slab of raw beef in front of a pack of starving lions. What did they think was going to happen?

The simple answer was to veto the thing. He was, after all, the boss now—the chairman—granted authority over all of the Wirtz companies, including the liquor distributorship, the banking arm, the insurance, farms and real estate holdings, as well as the Blackhawks, under a plan of succession devised by Bill's father, Arthur, the founder of the Wirtz Corp.

But despite an icy relationship with Peter, one that reached back to their boyhood days, Rocky felt obliged to grant the request, consequences be damned. As a senior vice president with the Blackhawks, Peter had been Bill's right-hand man, and had expressed an admiration for his father that bordered on worship. Many observers, in fact, assumed Peter, not Rocky, would take over the team. When Rocky shattered his brother's illusions, Peter's sense of anger and betrayal, while unspoken, radiated off of him like heat off a summer tarmac. *Fine*, Rocky said. *Go for it. But I don't think you're going to like the reaction.*

The choreography called for a red carpet to be rolled onto the ice and then the arena lights to be dimmed. Dale Tallon, the silver-haired general manager of the club and longtime loyalist to Bill, would step into a spotlight and read a few remarks. As he spoke, Bill's image would flash on the giant scoreboard overhead. Then, the moment Rocky felt was inviting trouble in an arena full of beered-up fans: a moment of silence.

At the appointed time, the Blackhawks players took to the ice and formed a circle under the scoreboard. The lights dimmed, casting the stadium in darkness save for a single spotlight into which Tallon stepped. Rocky watched the general manager lumber up to a set of microphones and adjust his reading glasses. Bill's face, as scripted, loomed on a set of rotating screens at the top of the scoreboard.

Tallon had not even begun when the first low rumble, like the signal of an approaching thunderstorm, rippled through the crowd. Catcalls and whistles came next, piercing the silence with angry shrieks. A chorus of jeers and chants rose. And then: BoooooOOOOOOO!!

"William Wadsworth Wirtz was a true Chicagoan," Tallon said, his words tinny and hollow. Boooooooooooo! "He loved this city and made enormous contributions to it"—BOOOOOOOoooooo!!!!—"of which we all can be proud." *BOOOOOOOOOOOOO!!!!*

Rocky glanced at Peter. His brother stood, arms folded, jaw set, in stoic silence. The faces of his sisters clouded, then ran with tears. *BOOOOOOOOOOOO!!!!!!*

Tallon gamely limped on, but by the time he finally asked for the moment of silence, the clamor was deafening.

Whatever slim hope Rocky had clung to that somehow, some way, things would not be as bad as he feared evaporated into the rueful reality that he had been absolutely right. The moment was not about healing, forgiveness; not about the commutation of a sentence banged down long ago on his father by heartsick, gavel-clutching fans. Bill Wirtz had helped build a franchise into a proud icon, yes, a team to make a kid knock the block off a kid from another town who favored the Flyers or the Penguins or the Rangers. But then he had forsaken it, turned it into a joke, for reasons they still couldn't fathom. Had he been another man—a kinder, more gracious person willing to admit his mistakes—he might have been granted leniency. But he was Bill Wirtz and—in their eyes—had committed his sin smugly, defiantly, arrogantly. Accordingly, the fans seized on the moment not to honor their tormentor, but to unleash decades of anguish in a single, ugly parting shot, purging their impotent frustration and howling at an owner who they believed had made a mockery of their devotion.

As the boos rumbled in a great, lusty wave through the arena, Rocky cycled through a range of emotions: anger, sadness, humiliation, disgust, helplessness. Then, like a skater hit with a breakaway pass, he felt a sense of calm descend. The team was his now and he would restore it and he would do so by any means necessary, including—and without prejudice—taking a wrecking ball to virtually every principle that his father had held sacred. Throughout his life, Bill Wirtz had made clear that breaking his commandments would be akin to blasphemy, that going against him would be like questioning God himself.

Rocky's response—forged in that moment and fashioned into a shining city of success in the astonishing years to come—embraced a similarly biblical fervor: So be it.

Worse Than It Seemed

The day after the United Center debacle, Rocky Wirtz paid his first official visit to Blackhawk offices at the arena. Though he had been around the team and indirectly involved for most of his adult life, his appearance marked one of the first times he had set foot in the franchise offices in more than two decades, the result of his father having all but excommunicated him from anything to do with team decisions. Rocky and his staff instead had worked in comfort and relative peace out of a suburban branch of the family liquor business in Wood Dale.

Given the years away from the United Center offices, Rocky scarcely knew what to expect as he trod the carpeted sanctum—regarding either the physical state of the offices or the economic condition and morale and makeup of the team itself, whose business operations were centered here. He had been counting on Peter to stay on as a senior vice president and provide this essential knowledge and guidance, but days after Bill's death, when Rocky told Peter that he would not be in charge of the team, the younger brother abruptly resigned. To Rocky's great relief, his brother assured him that he would help in any way he could during the transition, but in the days that followed it became clear that the promise was as empty as the United Center on most game nights. Peter did not reach out, did not debrief Rocky on anything—barely spoke to him, in fact, unless it was through attorneys.

In the dark about the franchise's inner workings, Rocky started with the one thing he did know: that the team's finances wobbled on shaky, possibly collapsing, ground. He'd gleaned as much from the Wirtz Corp.'s consolidated tax returns and, like the rest of the league, from a stunning comment Bill had made to the *Toronto Star* a few months before his death. The Hawks, Bill had told the newspaper, had lost some $191 million over ten years. The figure was shocking, but Rocky couldn't even trust that. Bill was known for crying poor. Yes, the Hawks were losing money, maybe a lot of money, but nearly $20 million *a year*? As Rocky began his tour of the United Center headquarters, he could only pray his father was exaggerating.

From the moment he stepped through the door, however, he knew better. The space was standard-issue insurance office—rows of cubicles bathed in fluorescent light, glassed-in enclosures for the front-office executives. Physically, at least, the space looked to be in good shape.

Something was off, however, a sense that grew on Rocky as he walked deeper in: other than a jangling phone, the Blackhawks' United Center offices were strangely quiet. Rows of cubicles sat empty. The back half of the office space stood unfinished, waiting for the growth that never came. While the other team that shared the arena, the Chicago Bulls, sprawled over two full floors, the Blackhawks took up barely half of one. At the desks that were occupied, Rocky noticed, the employees sat hunkered in silence. Who were they? What were they doing? And why, Rocky wondered, did no one look up when their new boss strode through the hushed floor?

As the phone continued to ring, Rocky poked his head in the office of Jimmy DeMaria, an executive who for some twenty-five years handled public relations for the team, but whose mouthful of a title—executive director of communications, broadcasting, and community outreach—struck Rocky as slightly extravagant. DeMaria had been one of Bill's untouchables—along with senior vice president and on-again, off-again general manager Bob Pulford and marketing chief Jim Sofranko.

On this day, DeMaria was the only front office person around, another oddity. "What's going on with the phones?" Rocky asked him. "Well, you know, we use interns—either from UIC or Loyola," DeMaria replied, according to Rocky's recollection. "Sometimes they have exams or they get in a fight with their boyfriend or girlfriend and don't show up."

"So who answers the phones?"

DeMaria shrugged. "It's OK. I'll answer it."

That wasn't the point, Rocky wanted to say, but let the moment slide. Later, he learned of an even more astounding phone issue: the listed number for ticket sales similarly went unanswered, though for a different reason—it was disconnected.

Rocky walked on, his disbelief growing. Everywhere he looked, he saw dysfunction. At one point, he asked where he could find some Post-it notes and a pad of paper. On someone's desk, he was told. "Why not in the supply closet?" *Let me guess*, he thought. *There is no supply closet.* How about a bottle of water? No. If Rocky was thirsty there was a water dispenser with paper cups in the corner.

A few days later, when Rocky called a 10:00 A.M. meeting of the Wirtz Corp. staff, he was astonished to see some of the employees saunter in ten, sometimes fifteen, minutes late. Gene Gozdecki, the beloved company lawyer on whom Rocky leaned heavily in the early days, explained the tardiness. "They never start the meetings on time," he told Rocky.

"Well, I always start meetings on time," Rocky answered. *There's no bottom*, he thought.

He realized how mistaken he was—and by what order of magnitude—when he got his first glimpse at the team's books. As Rocky had suspected, his father's claim that the team had lost $191 million in ten years was off. In the previous year alone, the team's financial vice president admitted, the Blackhawks had hemorrhaged $30 million *cash*. The team had a paltry 3,400 season ticket holders. It also had the NHL's second-lowest attendance and, at $44.84, the league's second-lowest average ticket price, higher only than the small-market Phoenix Coyotes.

One other bit of bad news, the VP told Rocky: in a week or so—barely two weeks into the season—the Hawks would be unable to make payroll.

“What?” Rocky said. It was true. In fact, the VP told him, “We’re actually $6 million in the hole.” A “capital call”—basically a cash infusion from Wirtz Corp.—had already been sent out.

Rocky was speechless. He’d always admired his father’s business savvy, and indeed Bill Wirtz had presided over the corporation as a whole with considerable success. But when it came to the Blackhawks in the last years of his life, it was as if he had given up. Or lost his way. Or lost his sense of priorities, micromanaging to the point that he couldn’t see the disaster unfolding before him. Or—in the case of not televising home games—he had fought public opinion for so long that he couldn’t see a way to give in and save face. Bob Verdi, the longtime *Tribune* columnist who would later be hired by the Blackhawks as the team’s official historian, theorizes that Bill simply could not bring himself to challenge the core principles of his own father, Arthur, no matter how outdated and disastrous the consequences. “One of Bill’s close friends—who needn’t be named—said to me once, ‘If Bill put the home games on TV, he thinks that Arthur would return from the grave and whip him,’” Verdi says. “I think there’s a lot to that. Arthur was a great businessman, but he was a hard-ass. You can’t underestimate his impact on Bill.

“Don’t forget,” Verdi adds, “there was a time when Arthur would not put the first period on radio because he didn’t want to give it away. The game would start at 7 o’clock, but the radio broadcast wouldn’t begin until 8:30.”

Of all the things that struck Rocky during that first United Center visit, the most puzzling was the state of neglect he saw in virtually every aspect of the franchise—from the quiet offices, to the lack of staff, to the lackadaisical attitude that seemed to permeate the entire operation like toxic mold.

Things weren’t much better at the Wirtz Corp. offices at 680 North Lake Shore Drive. The family business has called the esteemed address its home since the 1960s. Unlike the sleek skyscrapers forested around it, the stately edifice stands in stubborn old-school defiance, a throwback to a time of rich wood and plush leather boardrooms where men mulled the fates of their companies behind a curtain of cigar smoke. Once the largest commercial building in the world without a mortgage, the American Furniture Mart, as it was originally called, would later become known as the editorial headquarters for *Playboy*, the upstart gentlemen's magazine founded by a local man named Hefner.

Less conspicuously, the Wirtz family's sprawling conglomeration of real estate, banking, insurance, and liquor distribution occupied the nineteenth floor. Both Arthur and Bill had maintained offices there. Years before, "King" Arthur had commissioned designers to fashion an enormous round table for board meetings. Built of oak, with leather and glass inlays, the polished slab dominated an enormous corner office filled with a museum-worthy collection of English antiques, a glassed-in display case brimming with awards and honors, and a detailed replica of *The Blackhawk*, the 123-foot yacht Arthur helped design. "He would argue with the architects," Rocky recalls. "They would say something can't be done and he'd say, 'There's nothing that can't be done. Nothing's impossible—it just takes a little longer.'" Lest anyone doubt who was the real boss, framed photos of Arthur glowered down on the scene.

Rocky had visited his father's office at 680 before. But as he ventured in now, the austere feel of it struck him anew. A modest room at the end of a row of executive berths, it hardly seemed fitting for the chairman of Wirtz Corp. The space contained a nice antique work table, but the desk held only a couple of small drawers, and his secretary actually sat in the office with him.

Meanwhile, box after box brimming with thousands of letters and faxes and copies of those letters and faxes fired off by Bill in his last years rose in corners and under desks. For some reason Bill had demanded that the correspondence, including his own screeds to newspaper publishers, editors, and reporters, be preserved.

A clearer, if no less eccentric, explanation lay behind Bill's choice of digs, as Rocky knew. Bill had refused to occupy Arthur's far nicer office on the opposite end of the row either out of respect or, as Rocky has joked, because he felt Arthur might pay Bill a Marley-like visit one late night after everyone else had gone home. Indeed, when Rocky entered Arthur's office, it sat—save for a few stored boxes—just as it had when the King had reigned.

The rest of the floor seemed stuck in a time warp as well. Staffers clacked away on IBM Selectric typewriters, and a fax machine—"as big as a land mine," Rocky says—honked and screeched constantly, spitting out hot curling rolls of fax paper bearing letters, press releases, and official correspondence. "I said one of the first things we're going to do is get rid of that thing," Rocky recalls. "We could use it as an anchor or something."

To Rocky, the sorry state of affairs both at the United Center and at 680 was as heartbreaking as it was alarming. It was as if after decades of personally maintaining a pair of lovely homes—cleaning the gutters, patching cracks, replacing roof tiles, mowing the yard—the owner, Bill in this case, had begun to neglect all to the point that the amount of repairs needed was too overwhelming.

There was one other possible explanation, too sound to be discounted. Late in his life, Rocky and others say, Bill had begun showing signs of mental fogginess. "He was forgetting things," Rocky says. "He knew the city like a taxi driver, but he would get lost when he was driving." The family kept the father's condition under wraps, and Bill was still in charge. And when it came to the Blackhawks, he still trusted only his innermost circle, including Peter, DeMaria, and Bob Pulford. Everyone was hired and fired and respected, Rocky says, in exact proportion to their loyalty and little else. And for Bill, loyalty meant not questioning his decisions, no matter how damaging or ill-conceived. Those who held an opposing view, or who otherwise rebelled, or disagreed in any way, operated under the knowledge that while Bill could be generous, even indulgent, to those who obeyed, he could be ruthless to those who did not.

This despotic approach, to say nothing of Bill's stubbornness, seemed only to worsen as Bill's mental sharpness deteriorated. In his last years, Bill spent long hours writing letters upbraiding, hectoring, lecturing, and ripping everyone from reporters to publishers to family members to league officials, nursing grudges over matters embarrassingly petty, such as mildly critical articles from the city's newspapers.

He meanwhile clung to outmoded business practices that not only weren't working but were so clearly and obviously destructive that they defied both empirical evidence and logic. Somewhere along the line, for example, Bill had concluded that the only solution for the franchise was to cut expenses, including slashing vital staff and infrastructure spending, and player and coaching investment beyond a few splashy but ill-advised signings.

In the moment, however, the *why* of the team's plummet was far less important than *what now?* Rocky's mind flashed to the family's other businesses, namely the liquor distributorship he had run for nearly twenty years. He could tap resources from the corporation's strong balance sheet to stave off the team's immediate financial crisis, but that would be little more than applying a Band-Aid to a jugular wound.

Making matters worse was the nation's economic climate. In the fall of 2007, the clouds of a looming subprime lending hurricane were gathering over the nation in a giant, terrifying swirl. Relying on one family business to prop up another for any length of time in such an atmosphere would not just be foolhardy. It could be catastrophic—particularly given the Wirtz Corp. holdings in real estate, banking, and insurance, the three businesses most vulnerable to the nature of the coming crash. If the Blackhawks continued to burn through cash at the rate they were at the time—$20 million to $30 million *a year*—and those other holdings began to founder, it was not inconceivable that the entire enterprise, including the team that had been synonymous with his family's name for more than a half century, could be sucked under.

To the outside world, such a notion probably seemed ludicrous—the Wirtzes? They owned everything. So what if they borrowed a little from Peter to pay Paul? All the fans knew was that the team stunk as badly as it ever had and that the man who had just taken over bore the same last name as the guy who had led the Hawks to this precipice. Sure, there were musings in the papers that Rocky might be different—might at last be willing to make the kinds of changes that could restore the franchise to glory. But who knew? He'd been running the beverage side of the Wirtz enterprise. Did he know the first thing about hockey—about running a professional sports franchise? The guy who *did* know—Peter—was gone. Even if Rocky did have a clue, resurrecting a team like the Blackhawks would take a miracle of Lazarus-like proportions. And how likely was *that*? After all, he still had the biggest strike of all against him: his last name wasn't Halas or Jordan. It was, for hockey fans at least, the most despised name in Chicago: Wirtz.

For Rocky, the challenge frowned down on him as sternly as the framed visage of his grandfather, Arthur, staring onto the dusty and empty round table around which the old baron fashioned his now imperiled dynasty. In Arthur's day, the name Wirtz was something to be admired, the epitome of business royalty. Now . . .

There was so much Rocky didn't know, but one thing was certain. There was one person who would have been furious unto apoplectic at the state of affairs, a man convulsed with rage and determined to right the ship at all costs, sparing no one his wrath, granting no one quarter—no one, *no one*, be it a business associate, a fellow captain of industry, or, most assuredly, his own flesh and blood. You did not build a company the likes of Wirtz Corp. by being nice, and when you built it, you did not sustain it by sharing, or certainly not by ceding, power. Old school? Yes. Apologetic? Please.

He was who he was, a ruler supreme, the boss, the Chairman, the very essence of what was, perhaps, the most fitting of the many formidable nicknames given him during his eight-plus decades on this earth. And if you didn't know that upon first meeting him—who he was, what he was about—you learned quickly, and often painfully.

King Arthur

At six-foot-four, 340 pounds, with a voice that rumbled like a passing El train, Arthur Michael Wirtz, born in 1901, projected, by sheer physicality, a bearing so imposing that a mere glare of disapproval, a subtle rebuke delivered with icy-calm menace, could buckle the swagger of the most self-confident visitor. Even sitting behind his vast, empty desk, his dimensions somehow seemed to crowd the room. He had a habit of leaning slightly forward with a trembling tension that suggested, if sufficiently provoked, he might actually lunge at you. "He wasn't just big in the belly," recalls grandson Bruce Wirtz MacArthur, who was largely raised by Arthur and his wife, Virginia, after his own parents divorced, and who later went to work as Arthur's assistant. "I mean, the hands, the head . . . He wasn't verbose, but when he spoke, you got the message. You didn't want to go into the corner with him, as they say in hockey."

Bob Jordan, a lifelong friend of Rocky's, recalls another pal getting the full Arthur treatment when the young man started dating Arthur's granddaughter, Gail. "Arthur called him into the room and asked, 'Son, what are your intentions?' in that way he had," says Jordan. "Keep in mind, this was a seventeen-year-old kid who was simply having fun." Jordan's friend could barely croak out a response. "I can't really say," he finally managed. "I haven't given it much thought."

Arthur did have a softer side. When not darkened with anger, his broad, beefy face could appear open, even amiable. His eyes, peering out from behind horned-rim glasses, were often inscrutable—unless someone got off a good joke, in which case they wrinkled in pleasure.

Candid photos—of him cramming a hamburger into his mouth while sitting in the stands next to his old pal and business partner Jimmy Norris; of him posing on the ice in a suit and hockey gloves, clutching a stick being leapt over by Bobby Hull in full uniform; of him at his desk, chomping the end of a comically long stogie, Groucho Marx-style, while reading a circus program—suggest a not-so-closeted ham.

Small things could delight him. MacArthur recalls when Arthur brought home a newfangled gizmo called a radar range, the forerunner to the modern microwave. "We had one when no one else did," the grandson says. "And, oh, my God, Arthur was like a kid. It said don't put eggs in it because they would burst, so he immediately tested it and they exploded all over the kitchen."

And while he had a reputation for penny-pinching that would later find full expression in his son, Bill, he spared no expense when it came to his sartorial selections. Gold links clamped the cuffs of his custom-made shirts, satin, bespoke suits draped his ample frame. One snapshot, taken when he was probably in his thirties, shows Arthur posing in a banded straw hat, a merrily patterned tie cleaving a crisp white shirt, as he stands on the mobile gangway leading to an open-hatched TWA airliner.

The most telling hint of a latent sentimentality, however, comes in the form of a thick cache of love letters Arthur wrote to his eventual bride-to-be, Virginia Wadsworth. Bound into large plastic folders by Arthur's daughter Betty and featured in the elegantly appointed library room at the family's country estate, the letters gush and fret with the kind of teen angst and overheated prose you'd expect from the hopelessly lovelorn, but stun coming from the pen of a man who was often referred to by the imposing nickname Baron of the Bottom Line.

For the most part, however, Arthur Wirtz strode the world stage as the Chairman—unchallenged, undoubted, and undeniable—at work, at home, and at play. When he wanted something, Arthur Wirtz didn't ask, he ordered. People didn't question him, they scrambled to please him. "He wanted you at his beck and call," says MacArthur, who recalls being tethered to a pager the way a parolee wears an ankle bracelet. If he couldn't reach you, "he would chew your ass out."

And woe unto him who failed or even disappointed him, for he would bear a wrath as dreadful as Jehovah's. "I remember I was overdrawn once because my wife had done too much shopping," says MacArthur. "Arthur was furious. I said, 'It's her, not me.' He said, 'I don't care.' "

Nothing, however, infuriated the Baron of the Bottom Line more than bad news about the bottom line. Proof abounded, as one reporter, having been granted rare access to Arthur, discovered during a fraught meeting with a group of shareholders for the Chicago Milwaukee Corp. The group, which included other tycoons and business bigwigs, dared to question Arthur's solution for dealing with a bankrupt railroad in the company's portfolio. Forced to respond to the dissident rabble, Arthur, the non-salaried chairman of the publicly-held Chicago Milwaukee, promptly put down the insurrection with a tirade that could have made the needle of a Richter scale dance. "Wirtz's usually benign, hound-dog visage turned florid, and his 300-pound frame shook in anger," the reporter recounted in the 1979 *Chicago Tribune* profile. " 'Let's get the rudeness out of this meeting,' Wirtz roared," before admonishing "his adversaries on their lack of gratitude for management's performance in raising the company's earnings. Then he abruptly adjourned the meeting."

"I wanted to turn off their microphones," Arthur later growled to the reporter, "but they were all controlled by the same switch and I would have had to cut myself off, too."

Bruce MacArthur, in the same article, provided the unsurprising coda, spoken from experience: "He's a fair man," MacArthur told the reporter. "But if anyone tries to chisel him, God help him. He'll crucify them."

• • •

Rocky both witnessed—and suffered first degree burns from—the bubbling lava of Arthur's temper volcano while working his way up through the company to head the sprawling Judge & Dolph wine and beverage side of the family business. With alarming regularity, Rocky watched businessmen stride confidently into the Lake Shore Drive headquarters building of Wirtz Corp. only to see them slink out, hats in hand, pale, cowed, and talking to themselves after a face-to-face with the chairman.

Rocky himself recalls being "scared shitless" when called into "Grandpa's" famous office. "He could be charming or he could be the toughest s.o.b. in the world," Rocky says. "But no one was more intimidating, ever." Not even Rocky's notoriously bullying father, Bill, could withstand the withering glower of the Baron. "Dad was tough," Rocky says, "but he was a pussycat compared to my grandfather."

For all his physical intimidation, however, Arthur's true domination found expression in a much subtler form: psychological manipulation. "He was a master of mind games," says Rocky, "who seemed to take delight in the discomfort he could cause." One ploy, for instance, involved Arthur "putting the eraser side of a pencil in his mouth and aiming the point at you like he was pointing a gun," Rocky recalls. His eyeglasses served as another weapon. "He would go through this ritual," says Rocky. "He had reading glasses and regular glasses and he would keep taking one pair off and putting the other on, very deliberately while you just sat there and shut up."

Rocky remembers a typical visit to Arthur's professional lair—an experience that unfolded in much the same way, whether the visitor was a guest, a family member, or a hapless rival. The encounter would begin in the lobby of 680 North Lake Shore Drive, where Rocky could already feel the tension rising as he passed under the balefully stark gothic entrance of the elegant building. He'd announce his presence to the stone-faced and vaguely malevolent doorman, who would pass him off to the equally aloof elevator man, and the pair would clack together to the nineteenth floor. There, after coming to a juddering halt, the car would deposit Rocky onto a polished marble floor that led to a pair of glass doors framed in dark mahogany.

Before being granted an audience with the boss, Rocky would suffer an encounter with Gertrude Knowles, Arthur's secretary of fifty years. To Arthur and a highly curated list of friends and family, she was known as Gertrude. To everyone else, she was Mrs. Knowles, austere and forbidding. In a black dress, her hair primly bunned, she functioned as Arthur's surrogate, says MacArthur. When she told you to do something, you did it. "She may have been a woman in an era when men were running things, but I'll tell you one thing: you didn't mess with her."

Mrs. Knowles maintained three rolodexes on her desk and kept an identical set at home in case her boss called, which he invariably did—at all hours. Among her talents was her icy method for making supplicants cool their heels. Take a seat, she would say, her gelid demeanor all but foreclosing questions of how long it might be.

After a sufficient period, sometimes an hour or more, Arthur pressed a buzzer hidden under his desk alerting Mrs. Knowles to summon the victim. Nervous, irritable by now, perhaps perspiring a little, Rocky recalls that he would enter only to slam into a wall of frigid air. Arthur ran the air conditioning so low and hard, Rocky says, that when people smoked, they could see their cigarette burn down in the ashtray from the vent gusts. (One of the favorite family stories, impossible to prove, but telling nonetheless, involves a visit by Arthur to his doctor. During a routine physical, the physician was astonished to find that Arthur's blood pressure varied greatly between arms. As the story goes, the air conditioning blew so fiercely on one arm that Arthur's blood had literally been chilled.)

Placid and unflappable behind his spare desk, Arthur raised a guest's discomfort by blandly promising to be with him shortly. He would then pick up the phone and begin dialing. Depending on Arthur's mood, the number of calls could reach thirty or more before he slid off one pair of glasses, slipped on another, and peered at you in silence. Rocky recalls receiving the full treatment one afternoon when his grandfather summoned him to respond to a disappointing quarterly report. After the ritual wait, the grandson sunk into the chair facing Arthur—a chair always a few inches lower than his grandfather's—and eyed the neat stack of papers on Arthur's immaculate desk. The offending financial statements were not mentioned—though the incriminating document sat on top of the pile. Instead, Arthur said, "Mind if I make a few phone calls?" Ten became twenty became thirty, with Arthur occasionally excusing himself to go to the bathroom. The pattern continued, until Rocky found himself sitting alone for forty minutes or so. Finally, he poked his head into Mrs. Knowles's office. "Do you know when he's coming back?" he asked.

"Oh, he went to dinner a while ago," the secretary said. "He'll be back if you want to wait."

"His way of saying he was unhappy," Rocky explains.

The provenance of Arthur's imperiousness—to say nothing of his entrepreneurial genius—remains something of a mystery, though his childhood holds some clues. His father, Frederick, was a cop in Rogers Park, and his mother, Leona, a homemaker. Neither was known to be particularly harsh, and Frederick's job as a policeman suggests little appetite for riches or power. Arthur's stepmother, however, whom Frederick married after Leona died at a young age, loomed like a Disney movie villain, berating and belittling the boy mercilessly, according to a family member.

As for book learning, Frederick did recognize the value of a good education and strove to make sure Arthur and, later, his sister Esther, attended topflight private schools. And yet, the family was of such meager means that Arthur was forced to take a year off during high school to work to save money for college.

Less puzzling was the source of Arthur's indefatigable drive. His grandfather, Michael Wirtz, was born and raised in Luxembourg, the tiny nation wedged into the droplet of land bordered by France, Germany, and Belgium. Michael's father died just weeks after his birth, and in 1854, at age 20, Michael embarked at Havre, France, for a thirty-eight-day voyage across the Atlantic to a land shining with promise for many similarly situated young men. Indeed, in the period between 1830 and 1860, more than a million and a half Germans immigrated to America, the majority struggling farmers from Germany's southern region. Some sought to flee crippling agricultural reforms. Others hoped to escape the brutal droughts that had punished German farmers for generations. Still others simply sought opportunity in the sprawling American territories desperate for farmers who were willing to fight the privations of the landscape to cultivate and settle the land.

Decades before the robed, torch-bearing Statue of Liberty would rise as the then-tallest building in Manhattan, Michael's ship steamed into what was then the Port of New York (now New York Harbor) and disgorged its blinking immigrant passengers for processing. Having gained entry into the foreign land, Michael climbed aboard a steam train for the Midwest and settled in a small farm community about 45 miles northwest of Chicago. Fremont, Illinois, in the mid-nineteenth century still retained the kind of frontier exuberance typical of such Midwestern towns. A local newspaper, in fact, gushed in 1884 that the settlement sparkled as the "Gem of the Prairie," possessing an "equal quantity of prairie and timber—both of the best quality—well watered by streams and small lakes." Creaky wooden sidewalks, clip-clopping horses, a bustling post office, and a saloon where men could throw back a whiskey marked the town like the backlot for a Western talkie.

Michael first found employment as a $15-a-month farmhand and, through scrimping and government largesse, later procured a land grant for a small place of his own. Along the way, he wooed and married a German immigrant, a native of Hanover named Carolyn Hapke, and the two set to work building a homestead. Michael constructed a farmhouse and a barn and a paddock to keep the mules and horses. Carolyn busied herself with the growing family—eight children in all (a ninth died in infancy and a son, George, at nineteen years old). Fifth among the brood was Arthur's father, Fredrick.

Born in November 1866, Fred, as he was universally known, spent his youth and early adulthood working on the farm alongside his parents and siblings. Life in Fremont trundled slowly in those days. A trip into the city, for example, meant boarding a stagecoach for a teeth-jarring, three-hour expedition. Items from a local newspaper captured the essence of the small town pace in ways both funny and frightening. "Mr. Chas Beckwith's colts took a run while the driver shut the gate," fretted one blurb from the *Lake County Independent*. "The horses ran into Mr. Wirtz's corn crib and one fell down." Thankfully, the article concluded, "they were caught without much damage being done."

A more dramatic event occurred in 1897 when Fred, according to the *Independent*, was "injured [after] being struck by lightning." The paper noted that his older brother, John, a Fremont constable, rushed to his sibling's side and, to the relief of all, found "him better than they had feared."

Indeed, he recuperated enough that in 1899 he married and, in a break from family tradition, moved with his bride, Leona Miller, to the nearby big city, Chicago. The couple settled in the North Side Rogers Park neighborhood, taking up residence in a modest clapboard house at 1853 Morse Avenue, a home that Rocky recalls visiting and that still stands. Two years later, on January 23, 1901, the couple welcomed a son into the world, Arthur Michael Wirtz.

That same year, the man from whom Arthur took his middle name, his grandfather, Michael Wirtz, suffered a paralytic stroke and within days the family patriarch was gone. An obituary in the *Lake County Independent* described him as a man who was "one of the most prominent farmers in Fremont Township," a staunch Republican who had held assorted local political positions. "Widely known and universally respected and admired, he had become a dominant factor in the affairs of his community, political, social, and religious."

Michael may have been prosperous, but if there were riches to be had from his father's estate, it's clear Fred did not share in them. Indeed, indications are he lived his life as a farmer and a beat cop who struggled to make ends meet, a challenge heightened by the birth five years after Arthur of his sister, Esther. When Leona died in 1907, Fred remarried—a woman named Amanda Deegan—and the climate of the household changed. While Leona was known as gentle, Amanda was cruel, according to a family member. Her meanness may have been the precipitating factor behind Arthur heading off to military school.

Fred never advanced beyond high school and could scarcely afford to send his children to private academies. But to his credit, he recognized the importance of education and, with Arthur helping scrape together some money, found a way. For a time, the boy attended Armstrong grammar school in Rogers Park (now George B. Armstrong School of International Studies), then Northwestern Military Academy, at the time located in Highland Park. It was at age fourteen, however, that he was enrolled in the private school that would change the course of his life, Chicago's famed Francis W. Parker School in Lincoln Park. Named after its founder, Francis Wayland Parker, a Civil War veteran and a leader in the progressive school movement, the school proved more than an educational launching pad for Arthur. It's where he met the love of his life, a vivacious, effervescent, raven-haired beauty named Virginia Louise Wadsworth.

Hailing from a wealthy Edgewater family, Virginia proved a challenging conquest. The letters kept at the country estate suggest the teenager rarely missed a social event and enjoyed a large circle of friends, including a coterie of admiring boys seeking her favor. If she wasn't especially good at her studies (the letters include reference to her struggling to pass some of her classes), she unquestionably excelled in congeniality. A long list of young men, in fact, fairly swooned over young Virginia, several of them pouring out their feelings in the gushing, overwrought prose of the tortuously infatuated. Arthur was among them, and appeared to be the frontrunner in the Virginia sweepstakes but for a rival, an ardent and persevering admirer named Don, who seemed for a time to catch Virginia's eye.

Don was older, though, and when he went away for college, his absence seemed to provide an opening. Arthur wasn't able to take advantage. Burdened by the meager resources of his family, he was forced to take a year away from Parker to work for a telegraph company in Colorado. He "dug holes, worked on poles, and generally did hard labor," according to a summary of the letters prepared by Betty. "He appeared exhausted every evening."

Geographical distance forced both suitors to rely on the written word, and so they did. In a barrage of letters, complete with pet names, pleas for affection, and literary flourishes, they lavished Virginia with attention. "I have not heard from you," Don agonized in one letter. "I am so lonely for you."

"It is one day short of four weeks since I've heard from you," countered Arthur, "and I hope I will never have to go through such a terrible time again. I miss you terribly much. At times it is almost unbearable."

Also buried in one of Arthur's letters is an admission of self-doubt that, like his somewhat syrupy declarations of love, would have shocked anyone who encountered the swagger of the famously domineering and imposing King Arthur in later life. "My Darling Sweetheart," he wrote. "I am very proud thinking my sweetheart is doing so well [in school]. I wish I could make you proud of me also, but I don't think I will." In the annals of prophecy, it is hard to imagine a less prescient lament as evidenced even then by Arthur's quick recovery from whatever momentary doubt he harbored about himself.

Virginia, having graduated from Parker, simply stopped responding to Don's letters and, after numerous unrequited pleas, the would-be Lancelot abandoned the field to the triumphant Arthur, who basked in the increasingly warm correspondence from his fair Virginia to the point that he asked for her hand in marriage.

Even then, one last hurdle—this one more Romeo and Juliet than Arthurian—stood in the couple's way. Virginia's parents, who had built a fortune in the stock market, regarded the son of a police officer as something less than an appropriate match for their debutante daughter. Whereas Arthur's father walked a beat and climbed into overalls to work the farm on weekends, the Wadsworths dressed for dinner and ate off fine china ferried to and from their table by white-coated help. Virginia's father sported a monocle and her mother, like Virginia herself would in later days, favored fashionable bonnets and wore white gloves outside of the home. Accordingly, when Arthur chose to attend the University of Michigan in Ann Arbor, they pounced. They sent Virginia to the University of Colorado with the hope that the couple would come to their senses and forget any further marriage nonsense.

Fate in the form of a more powerful maternal figure—Mother Nature—intervened. The Rocky Mountain climate, it turned out, proved detrimental to Virginia's constitution, and barely a year into her studies she fell victim to a serious bout of pneumonia that left her laid up for weeks and longing to escape the thin air. She hastened back to Chicago and, after sufficiently recovering, enrolled at Northwestern University to pursue a degree at the School of Commerce (later known as the Business School). Virginia loved everything about the college—its scenic perch on Lake Michigan, the gothic buildings strewn across the manicured green quadrangles, her refreshing independence at the sorority where she lived—and indeed her embrace of the school would begin a family connection that would span generations, down to her grandson, Rocky.

While Virginia flourished in Evanston, Arthur languished at Michigan. "There's no place to go in Ann Arbor," he complained to her in one letter. "I don't believe I would advise any girl to go to [here], although I would love to have you go just to have you with me."

He endured, however, and after graduating the university in 1922, he returned to Chicago and he and Virginia resumed their courtship where their letters had left off. Arthur quickly secured a job as an assistant surveyor on a railroad. Now gainfully employed, if not exactly on the path to riches, Arthur finally won reluctant approval from Virginia's parents to marry their princess.

So it was in February 1926 that an engagement notice appeared on the front page of the *Chicago Evening American*'s society page. The announcement trumpeting the impending marriage of the "daughter of Mrs. Charles Wadsworth of 4880 Sheridan Road to Arthur M. Wirtz of Rogers Park" featured a portrait sketch of Virginia—the dark-ringleted, porcelain-faced image made to look like an engraving on a brooch. The couple was married on March 7, 1926, in the chapel of Fourth Presbyterian Church on Michigan Avenue, beginning a relationship with that landmark place of worship that, as with Northwestern University, would endure for the rest of his life.

Though Arthur enjoyed working on the railroads (many years after making his fortune he would tell people he was a railroad man at heart), he burned with far larger ambitions. As would become clear soon enough, one of his great strengths lay in his ability to size up people and opportunities. One young man whom he admired greatly was a friend from Parker named Arthur Rubloff. In the years since the two men had attended, Rubloff had built a name for himself in real estate, a field in which Arthur's father had dabbled. After showing Arthur the ropes, Rubloff helped Arthur hang out his own shingle in the mid-1920s. Rubloff would go on to become one of the country's most successful real estate moguls and the driving force behind the commercial and retail explosion along Chicago's North Michigan Avenue. His pal Arthur, as it turned out, would become one of the few men with a net worth nearly as astounding, if not in some ways more so.

In the twenties, however, Arthur's journey was just beginning. With $10,000 in capital, he partnered with two New York realtors, W. Francis Little and Rolland E. Huburt, in 1927. The trio headquartered their operation at 3152 Sheridan Road, across from Belmont Harbor.

Initially, their primary property was a new sixteen-story apartment building at 534 Stratford Place in Chicago's Lake View neighborhood. But it wasn't long before the firm of Wirtz, Hubert, & Little counted nearly eighty buildings and some three thousand rental units among their assets. The majority of those structures and dwellings rose along the North Side lakefront, where Arthur and Virginia would maintain their primary residence.

Just as they were establishing themselves, however, the Great Depression slammed into the nation's economy like a category five hurricane. Fortunes were swept away overnight. The entire financial system, from Wall Street to Chicago's famed Board of Trade, staggered on the brink of collapse. Housing values plummeted. Retailers abandoned large commercial spaces. Sheriffs tossed people from their homes as bread lines stretched out of churches and shelters. Among the victims were Arthur's in-laws, the Wadsworths. Having looked down their noses at him only a few years before, Virginia's parents now found themselves having to turn hat in hand to their increasingly prosperous son-in-law, as they were unable even to make house payments. By all accounts, Arthur did not hesitate, nor did he hold the humbling reversal of fortunes over their heads. He took them in and the subject was rarely raised again.

He could afford to be magnanimous. While his in-laws lost everything in the market crash, Arthur had placed his bets with more tangible assets—purchased with as little debt as possible. "Everybody owed the banks one million, two million dollars," he would tell the *Chicago Sun-Times* many years later. As luck would have it, Arthur's firm could not be foreclosed on because he didn't owe anybody. Most importantly, having sunk his proceeds into gold, he possessed huge reserves of cash in the ultimate buyer's market. He also took full advantage of a particular skill he had developed early in his career, one that was ideal in the throes of a depression: a shrewd faculty for rescuing highly leveraged building corporations and their assets by slashing their debt loads deeply, enough to keep them out of the hands of receivers.

Among those impressed by Arthur's growing reputation was another opportunistically astute businessman, a Canadian who had earned his own renown as a grain speculator on Chicago's Board of Trade.

James E. Norris—"Pop," as he would come to be known—was born in 1879 in Montreal, the heir to a family fortune built through ownership of mills, land, and a fleet of ships. Pop Norris, whose family lived in Windsor across the border from Detroit, arrived in Chicago by way of his father, James, who had moved Norris Grain Inc. to 141 Jackson Boulevard when the son was eighteen. Within ten years, the younger Norris was president of that firm as well as Norris Cattle Company, which boasted three of the nation's largest cattle ranches. At the age of thirty, he began buying grain elevators, an investment that would soon vault him to distinction as the world's largest cash grain buyer. By 1940, he had an estimated wealth of $200 million.

Like Arthur, though two decades his senior, Pop Norris dressed the part of buttoned-up industry captain, draping himself in somber but finely-cut custom suits, a horseshoe of dark hair framing a round face that, in the few snapshots extant, featured a stern, even gruff, expression.

When the Depression struck, Norris, also like Arthur, sat flush and ready to buy. Tapping the firm's ample cash reserves, he gobbled up luxury properties being unloaded by cash-strapped Chicago owners for pennies on the dollar. One acquisition involved a parcel of prime real estate at Randolph and Michigan. To broker the deal, Norris turned to the firm headed by the young man he had been hearing so much about. Arthur delivered. Impressed by the young man, Norris proposed going in on an apartment building at 1420 North Lake Shore Drive, a luxury high-rise that boasted a commanding view of the lake in the prized Gold Coast neighborhood. If amenable, Arthur would be both an investor and the property's overseer. Leaving his old firm behind, Arthur leapt at the chance, and formed a new partnership.

Different in age, temperament, and relative social pedigree, on the surface the men seemed an unlikely match. But Arthur and Pop Norris clicked both professionally and personally, each contributing his own strengths. Arthur assumed the role of the tough negotiator; Norris supplied his unerring eye for undervalued properties along with a keen sense of timing. On one principle they both agreed: avoid highly leveraged purchases—any deal that involved borrowing large sums and any loans that carried high interest rates. In a business climate where cash was not only king but the queen, the court, and the palace as well, they thus not only survived the Depression, they conquered it. Within the space of a decade, in fact, the partners strode the nation's economic stage as two of the richest men in the country and something approaching royalty in Chicago.

At home, meanwhile, Arthur took his place as head of another enterprise: his own family. A year after their marriage, he and Virginia gave birth to their first child, a girl they named Cynthia. A year later came a son, William Wadsworth Wirtz, soon to be known as Bill or Billy. In 1934, another son was born, Arthur Michael Wirtz Jr., followed in 1936 by a second daughter, Elizabeth "Betty" Wirtz. Virginia, whom Arthur called "Queenie," stayed home with the children. The King himself, brandishing Excalibur, charged headlong into the creation of an empire.

"Real Estate, Skates, and Fists"

The dynasty that ultimately would arise from the new Wirtz and Norris alliance may have risen from a foundation of sports arenas and hockey teams, but when it came to how the men regarded those essential materials they differed drastically. Though Arthur was something of a sportsman—an accomplished horseman, an avid fisherman, and a man who swam laps most every morning—he cared little about the proletarian world of professional sports. To him, franchises were a means to an end; fans were customers. His passions, to the extent they were aroused, rose and fell on the cold calculation of profits, losses, and margins. If a team in which he invested won, fine—as long as the turnstiles kept spinning and the cost of assembling such a team comported with a healthy bank account.

Norris was the opposite. He adored sports—hockey in particular—which he played (along with squash and tennis) in his youth and during his college years at McGill University. Growing up in hockey-mad Montreal, he followed his favorite teams with the starry-eyed fervor of the most ardent fan and the dream to one day own his own team. But buying a franchise wasn't enough. He wanted to win, so that when his dream was realized he opened his wallet wide, bottom line be damned.

But what might have been irreconcilable differences in any other partnership raised scarcely a ripple on the lake of this particular collaboration. The beauty of their merger, in fact, owed to their opposing approaches. "Mr. Norris saw in Arthur a sharp young fellow who could help him make money in real estate; Arthur saw a man who had several millions in cash," a close associate told the *Wall Street Journal* in a profile many years later. One of their first acquisitions, for example, came in 1933 with the purchase of the Detroit Olympia stadium. With the city still reeling from the Depression (between 1929 and 1931, automobile production had plummeted by a third and unemployment in Detroit had shot up from nineteen thousand to more than two hundred thousand; the Depression, in fact, hit Detroit harder than any other big city in the United States, according to census figures), the arena's owners were desperate to unload the $2.5 million facility, already in receivership after only six years, at ten cents on the dollar. For another $100,000, they'd even throw in the hockey team, then known as the Falcons, of the fledgling National Hockey League. For Arthur, grabbing a prestigious property at such a deep discount was a sound investment on the merits. For Norris, the chance to own the stadium *and* rescue the floundering team was beyond what he could have hoped. The partners pounced, renamed the team the Red Wings, and with Arthur handling the business end, Pop Norris, and his son, James D. "Jimmy" Norris, instantly remade the franchise into one of the league's premiere franchises.

Two years later, the partners, with the increasing presence of Jimmy Norris, staged an even bigger coup, seizing control of what was, at the time, the largest indoor stadium in the world: Chicago Stadium. About four miles due west of the Loop, the arena rose at 1800 West Madison—hunkered may be more accurate—as "a technical masterpiece of construction," according to a 1929 souvenir program commemorating the event. Occupying a full city block, it featured classic Greek architecture, including panels depicting "heroic friezes" of athletes and sporting contests, and held 8,000 more seats than Madison Square Garden. Fans filled every one on opening night, March 28, 1929, for a boxing match between world light heavyweight Tommy Loughran of Philadelphia, and world middleweight champion Mickey Walker of New Jersey. The owner of the $7 million stadium, Patrick T. "Paddy" Harmon, who purportedly sank $2.5 million of his own money to bring his brainchild to fruition, raked in an indoor record $187,000 in gross receipts that night. (The evening wasn't an unqualified success. In what perhaps was an omen of problems to come, though one with a comic twist, the still-unfinished roof caught fire as the two fighters fought. The fire department descended on the building. Water "poured through the roof and showered the spectators, panic being avoided through the efforts of Andy Frain ushers who calmly informed complaining members of the crowd that the shower was caused by uncouth persons spitting from the balconies," the *Albany Ark Times* recounted in a story several years later.)

The Stadium survived the night and soon the "palace," as Harmon liked to call it, was playing host to everything from the National Football League's first playoff game (yes, indoors, on a field sixty yards long between goal posts) to the 1932 Democratic National Convention that nominated Franklin Roosevelt. Nine months after its opening, the Madhouse on Madison, as it would come to be known, also became home for the city's hockey team—the Chicago Black Hawks. (Originally spelled as two words, the name took its current form in 1986 after Bill Wirtz discovered the one-word spelling in some original franchise documents.)

To the consternation of the partners, however, particularly Norris, the hockey franchise was merely renting space. Several years earlier, Norris had bid on the team, but had lost out to a syndicate headed by a former Harvard football star and Boston Brahmin named Huntington Hardwick. At the time, hockey was a novelty in the states, professional play having made its way south from Canada only a couple of years prior. (The *Chicago Tribune* admitted as much in its coverage of the first game in Chicago: "To most Chicago sports fans, hockey is new. Comparatively few of the audience [are] able to distinguish the fouls, penalties, or brilliant plays of the team, but with the address system the promoters of the famous Canadian sport hope to educate the fans rapidly.")

The National Hockey League had been formed in 1917, but the first American franchise—in Boston—wasn't established until 1924. New York and Pittsburgh added teams in 1925. The NHL wanted Chicago to be next, but league officials wanted the right owner. They thought they had found him in Hardwick. To fill the roster, his syndicate brokered a deal to buy the Portland Rosebuds of the Western

Hockey League for $100,000 and seemed set to launch the expansion team into a new season. After only a month, however, and for reasons unclear, Hardwick's group wanted out.

As luck would have it, they found a buyer in an eccentric tycoon named Frederic McLaughlin. Heir to his father's successful coffee business—McLaughlin's Manor House—the sixty-one-year-old Chicago native, another Harvard graduate, lived a life of leisure. Stiff spined, mustachioed, and something of a dandy, McLaughlin had no experience in the ice hockey business. Instead, his claim to fame was his service as commander of a machine gun unit during World War I, so much so that he insisted that people address him as "Major," even in civilian life. In buying the Chicago franchise, he was certain he could capitalize on the long, fierce rivalry between New York and the Second City.

McLaughlin's first task was to give the team a name. For that, he turned—as he did in so many aspects of his life—to his military service. His outfit had been the 333rd Machine Gun Battalion of the 85th Division—nicknamed "Black Hawk" after a Sauk Indian chief who had battled government troops over the incursion of white settlers into former tribal lands in Illinois. The major loved it. To create a logo, McLaughlin prevailed upon his wife, a thrice-married former Broadway dancer and silent-film star named Irene Castle. Her design—the profiled head of a Native American chief enclosed in a black circle—is regarded to this day as one of the premier insignias in all of sport (though, like other Native American images associated with teams, it has also had its share of detractors).

In their new sweaters, with their new owner, the team debuted on November 17, 1926, becoming one of what later was known as the NHL's Original Six franchises (with Toronto, Montreal, Boston, New York, and Detroit). It was an auspicious start. The Blackhawks and their opponent, then known as the Toronto St. Patricks, took the ice before a capacity crowd of 8,000 (7,200 seated and 800 standing) at the Chicago Coliseum—a former Virginia prison torn down and reassembled at the corner of Wabash Avenue and Fourteenth Street. "When the opening whistle was blown, the Hawks dashed out and unloosed a sustained attack on the Toronto goal net," according to the next day's account in the *Chicago Tribune*. Between periods, "fancy skaters" took to the ice, to entertain the crowd. When the final whistle sounded, the Blackhawks had thumped the "Toronto sextet" 4–1.

The promise of that night, however, faded quickly. The team finished 19–22–3 (wins, losses, and ties) that first year and fared poorly the next, despite McLaughlin employing the kind of gimmick that years later would have delighted another Chicago eccentric, Chicago White Sox owner Bill Veeck. McLaughlin plucked a deep-voiced jewelry auctioneer from Saskatchewan to serve as cheerleader.

In the eighteen-year McLaughlin era, the team became known for three things: firing coaches, bickering with the league, and mediocrity. The Blackhawks did win two Stanley Cups—in 1934 and 1938. But even the 1938 champs suffered a dismal regular season record of 14–25–9. It remains, to this day, the team with the worst regular-season record of any Stanley Cup champion.

Despite the Hawks' struggles, Norris wanted the team as desperately as McLaughlin delighted in keeping it from him, turning down one entreaty after another. Norris retaliated by charging nettlesome fees and creating scheduling difficulties.

Arthur was more bemused than upset. Sure, he would like to control the Blackhawks—anything to fill the seats. At the time, however, he was far more interested in other enterprises, including adding new buildings to the Wirtz Corp. portfolio (in all of which Norris had a stake) and finding ways to fill his stadiums with something besides sweaty, demanding athletes. He bought the massive American Furniture Mart, which in time would become the 680 North Lake Shore Drive building where Wirtz Corp. would be headquartered. He and Pop Norris snapped up the landmark Bismarck Hotel in downtown Chicago. The partners also acquired a collection of other arenas, including big halls in St. Louis, Indianapolis, and Omaha.

Filling the seats of Chicago Stadium with profit-generating attractions proved harder than Arthur had anticipated. Hosting conventions was nice, but not exactly lucrative. Blackhawks' crowds—if you could call them that—dropped off sharply after the initial interest and anyway, paid far less for tickets than other acts. Rodeo competitions drew decent, if not packed, houses. Boxing showed promise—and indeed would in time deliver a gate receipt knockout for the duo. But Arthur needed something immediately, something different and sensational. But what? Or who?

• • •

In the 1924 Winter Olympics, a blonde Norwegian skater with a pixie face, Glinda the Good Witch locks, and Shirley Temple charisma tightened her laces and glided onto the ice. A mere eleven years old, Sonja Henie did not perform well that day. During her program, she abandoned her choreography several times to consult with her coach, a serious breach of the rules. Not surprisingly, she finished dead last out of the eight skaters competing. But Henie took it in stride. Even at that tender age, she seemed to know that she was destined for stardom and, the judges that day aside, few people who knew the precocious child had cause to doubt that would indeed be the case. The primary reason was her parents. Both her father, Wilhelm Henie, a prosperous Norwegian furrier, and her mother, Selma Lochman Nielsen, wealthy by inheritance, set about providing everything the girl would need to rise to the top. When she first set blade to ice at age eight, for example, the parents already had her on a special diet and paired with the best coach money could buy. Already a prodigy by age ten, Henie developed her signature grace by training with a famous Russian ballerina of the day, Tamara Karsavina (the training accounts for the nickname given her later in life: the Pavlova of the ice, after Anna Pavlova, the Russian prima ballerina who made famous the dying swan). Three years after her unfortunate Olympic debut, she won her first figure skating world championship at age fourteen. She proceeded to win the next ten in a row, a feat that to this day has not come close to being repeated. During that period, she also collected three gold medals in three consecutive Olympics—in 1928, 1932, and 1936—another figure skating achievement yet to be repeated.

Her impact on the sport, however, transcended mere championships. Having grown into a toothsome young woman, she was the first figure skater to wear a short skirt and white skating boots, both of which, while slightly scandalous at the time, were adopted as the standard look for the sport. Her unique performance style also transformed the sport. Rather than skate to a spot and execute a jump, then skate to another and jump again—the approach of most competitors at the time—Henie drew on her ballet training to incorporate dance choreography to her routines, filling them with elegance, fluidity, and theatricality. Her innovations elevated what had once been an also-ran event to one of the premier competitions in the Winter Olympics.

But skating turned out to be only the beginning of her career. Abandoning her amateur status after her third Olympic gold medal, she took up acting and live-show performances. Darryl Zanuck, the legendary Hollywood studio chief, having caught one of her exhibitions in Los Angeles, immediately recognized her star power and signed her to a lucrative film contract. A splashy 1939 *Time* magazine cover featured her seated in a director's chair, legs stretching down to her signature white boots, the cover punctuated with a prescient, if slightly brash, quote from Henie: "Most always, I win."

It was around that time that Arthur, by happenstance, attended a small, unpublicized amateur figure skating exhibition booked into the Stadium. Stunned by the turnout—eleven thousand people for a show with no big names and little theatrical flourish—he tried unsuccessfully to book a second performance. When the amateurs refused, Arthur mounted a show of his own, headlining it with professional skaters that included two—Eddie Shipstad and Oscar Johnson—who were performing a sort of vaudeville ice routine to packed houses at a Chicago nightclub.

The show turned a tidy $25,000 profit. Arthur—"a sensitive feeler of the turnstile pulse," as a *Milwaukee Journal* reporter described him—rightly sensed a huge moneymaker, to say nothing of a way to fill his newly acquired stadium.

To create the kind of extravaganza he envisioned, however, turned on signing the biggest name of the day: Henie. Prevailing upon a friend to travel to Scandinavia as his proxy, Arthur put out a feeler gauging the sensation's willingness to make a deal.

A few weeks later, she boarded a plane bound for America with a signed contract to perform eight shows at $3,000 a performance. The run, which played to a capacity crowd every night, launched a phenomenon the likes of which amazed a nation. Emboldened by the Chicago triumph, Arthur brought the show to a far bigger stage—New

York—where Henie again wowed spellbound audiences, raking in an $80,000 profit for Arthur in the process.

Thrilled again by the response, Arthur, now Henie's theatrical manager and agent, bankrolled an extravaganza built around her, and in 1937, the Hollywood Ice Revue was born. Over the next four years, she toured the country, playing to record crowds, including at the Detroit and Chicago stadiums. The crowning point came in 1940, when the managing director of Rockefeller Center's prestigious Center Theater agreed to spend a quarter of a million dollars turning the venue into an ice theater specially designed for Henie. The production itself, patterned after the Ziegfeld Follies, cost some $300,000, an enormous sum at the time. Despite Henie's uninterrupted string of successes, no one, including Arthur, could say with certainty whether such a lavish spectacle would be fabulous or a flop. This was Center Theater in the heart of Broadway, whose audiences arrived in fur stoles and dripping diamonds, not the Madhouse on Madison buzzing with beer-soaked factory workers roaring during hockey fights.

The verdict came on October 10, 1940, when the revue opened to a full house and critical raves. "It Happens on Ice" delighted audiences for ten years and smashed box office records, more than doubling in some cases the take of the biggest Broadway hits running nightly a few blocks away (*Oklahoma!* to cite but one example, pulled in $30,000 to the Henie show's $80,000).

In all, Wirtz's Henie shows played before more than 6.3 million people over the years, bringing its star at one point an unfathomable $2 million annual salary. Side deals, including endorsement contracts and products such as skates, clothing, jewelry, dolls, and other merchandise that bore her name, added yet more riches. At one point, according to the society pages of the day, she and Arthur even went in on a restaurant, a short-lived endeavor, but one that demonstrated her incredible reach as well as her growing closeness to Arthur and the entire Wirtz family. Indeed, he and Henie made numerous globe-trotting treks—some with Virginia along and some without. ("Mother was challenged, I think, with Sonja Henie being such a beautiful ice skater," says Arthur's lone surviving child, Elizabeth "Betty" Wirtz. "She never went anywhere unless my dad invited her.") They even made a voyage to Henie's home in Norway. "This place was magnificent," says Bruce Wirtz MacArthur, who was named Henie's godson and who went along. "There must have been two hundred steps to reach it from the fjord."

Henie wasn't the only one to cash in on her name. Arthur achieved a measure of fame as well, as the Father of the Ice Revue. That owed partly to another example of him being ahead of his time: his use of the yet-to-be-coined term "branding." To wit, he insisted that all promotional materials connected to Henie or her shows include the phrase "Arthur Wirtz presents." (Arthur would employ the same tactics with Blackhawks' radio broadcasts, which were introduced with the words "Arthur Wirtz and the Blackhawks present . . .")

The kicker was that the whole thing was a sort of glorious accident. Arthur never had the slightest desire to become an entertainment mogul. "I'm just a real estate man trying to make a living," he once told the *Wall Street Journal.* "I make a good deal once in a while, but I make two bad ones for every one of those." He simply wanted to make his investments pay off, which meant finding ways to fill arena seats. But the Henie bonanza, for example, inspired other quirky ventures, including an ill-fated partnership with the famed Western film star Hopalong Cassidy. According to a 1953 article in the *Milwaukee Journal* that bore the headline "Real Estate, Skates, and Fists," Arthur had read somewhere that Cassidy was so wildly popular that three hundred thousand people lined the streets of New York City, hoping to catch a glimpse of him riding his horse. A few days later, the article reported, Wirtz found himself caught in a traffic jam caused by the very same cowboy actor making a live appearance. "You don't have to be a genius to put that behind turnstiles," Arthur told the newspaper. And indeed, after luring Cassidy away from other commitments, Arthur made the movie star the headliner in a circus he had created as a showcase. The results were stunning. The show generated a quarter of a million dollars in profit in Chicago and another $30,000 in Detroit. His sudden status as a skating and circus impresario "makes Arthur Wirtz one of the oddest real estate men who ever hired Hopalong Cassidy," the *Journal* quipped. Arthur miscalculated, however, in his next move. He took the circus east. To be sure, Cassidy was well known there, as evidenced by the massive turnout in Manhattan, but the tour flopped, consuming the earlier profits and adding a loss of $220,000 more. "I still can't figure out what happened," Arthur told the paper.

He suffered no such headaches with Henie, however, which brought a windfall large enough for him and Norris to pay off the Chicago Stadium with millions to spare. It also positioned Arthur and Norris to continue their highly calculated but prolific buying spree. For Arthur, that meant widening the reach of the Wirtz Corp., as it was now known, beyond luxury apartment towers, furniture marts, and sports arenas.

Pinpointing the right sector didn't take long. After the repeal of Prohibition in 1933, the pent-up demand for alcohol gushed like a ruptured dike. Chicago proved particularly thirsty, with corner bars dotting every neighborhood and a booming dining trade—not to mention the parched throats at sporting events. Arthur, in yet another example of business prescience, bellied up to the opportunity. He started small, buying a Milwaukee-based distributor, the Edison Liquor Company, in 1941. He then searched for undervalued companies—mom and pop operations eager to cash out. One by one, Arthur built a network of distributors, folding each into Wirtz Corp., with Norris getting a piece.

In 1945, Walgreen Drug Co., another burgeoning Chicago-based corporation, announced it was selling a liquor wholesaler named Judge & Dolph. Founded as a pharmaceutical firm in 1890 in St. Louis—but one with a liquor license as well—Judge & Dolph converted to a liquor wholesaler in Illinois with the repeal of Prohibition. By the time Walgreens had put it up for sale, it was one of the largest businesses of its kind in the state. For Arthur, Judge & Dolph met several crucial needs: First, it quenched his thirst for diversification. Second, it vaulted Wirtz Corp.'s new beverage division to the top of the Illinois liquor trade. As with Sonja Henie, the move was a masterstroke. Judge & Dolph, operating under the Wirtz aegis, didn't just supplement the corporation. It became a cornerstone. Within ten years, the company boasted a capital and surplus of $2.5 million, and three branches in Chicago, Waukegan, and Aurora, Illinois. In 1956, Arthur, as chairman of the board of directors, cut the ribbon on a brand-new, 95,800-square-foot warehouse and headquarters at 2037–81 Clybourn

Avenue. ("Celebrities of stage, screen and the sports arena, together with thousands of Chicago and Chicago Suburban liquor licensees, were feted and entertained" at a two-day dedication event, according to a special issue of the *Illinois Beverage Journal.*)

• • •

While Arthur raised a glass to the new venture, Norris focused on his passion: hockey. Unfortunately for him at the time, Americans did not share his fervor in large numbers. The sport, in fact, remained a niche league throughout the 1940s and 1950s, with economic trouble bad enough to force the Norris family to invest millions to prop it up. That largesse, paid without hesitation by Norris, would earn both Pop and his son Jimmy a spot in hockey's Hall of Fame.

Even so, Pop Norris continued to hound Major McLaughlin to relinquish control of the Blackhawks right up until the coffee baron's death in 1945. Finally given his chance, Norris, however, encountered a glitch. Because he owned a stake in other NHL teams he could not buy the Blackhawks outright. Instead, he coaxed longtime Hawks President Bill Tobin to front a syndicate that took over as de facto owners. Jimmy Norris and Arthur were part of the group, but Pop Norris called the shots. Paradoxically, after such a long battle, Pop seemed to neglect the team in favor of his beloved Detroit Red Wings. "He didn't really care about Chicago or New York, so he would have all the good players funneled to Detroit," Rocky recalls. Predictably, the Blackhawks continued to dwell at or near the bottom of the standings.

Enter Jimmy Norris. Rich, flashy, handsome, brash, he strutted onto the sporting world stage the way he swaggered into clubs: with his jet-black hair slicked back, a Cuban cigar hooked between the crook of two fingers, a girl on each arm, and a slap on the back for the proprietors. Indeed, where the elder Norris operated with the kind of button-downed, fusty sense of propriety expected at the time of the scion of a great fortune, the son plied his trade as an archetypal bad boy.

One story stands in for many in capturing his rogue reputation. In his younger days, Jimmy had been sent to Yale, but, chafing at the discipline of Ivy League academia, he later claimed he'd bribed the bursar to send Pop Norris doctored grades while Jimmy and his chauffeur "went around the country looking for dice games," Rocky says. "He would wind up in crap games with the potato farmers in Idaho." The scam worked for three years until Pop became wise. But that hardly slowed Jimmy. He floated around town, his pants pockets bulging with money clips clamping thousands in crisp one-hundred-dollar bills. He stashed more stacks in the vest pockets of his silk-lined suit jackets. He lavished the cash on maître d's and coat-check girls and waitresses who caught his eye. "He would go to tip the bellhop and a couple of hundreds would fall out," Rocky recalls.

He was, in short, "a classic man's man," Rocky says. "He drank, he gambled." He also had good, if undisciplined, business instincts. Worried about his son's baser proclivities, Pop prevailed upon Arthur to keep an eye on the young playboy. "Jim was a charming guy who loved having a good time and hanging around with the sort of people who frequent race tracks and prize fights," the *Wall Street Journal* wrote in 1972, quoting a close associate. "The old man saw he needed someone to keep [Jimmy] from spending every cent he had."

After a while, the reporter wrote, "Jim rarely made a move without clearing it with Arthur. If it wasn't for Arthur, God knows what would have happened to Jim."

Arthur not only didn't begrudge Jimmy his vices and swagger—he admired them. Why someone like the Baron of the Bottom Line, who delighted in dominating most anyone in his orbit, got such a kick out of a character like Jimmy remains something of a mystery. Perhaps the somewhat starched Arthur enjoyed living vicariously through his footloose counterpart, who, though younger than he by only five years, seemed at times like a mischief-loving teenager. Perhaps Jimmy's ability to mix business and pleasure, his full and hedonistic embrace of life, may have intrigued a man who devoted his life to self-discipline and moral rectitude.

Whatever the case, the pair hit upon a division of labor that made for a partnership at least as formidable as the pairing of Arthur and Pop. While Arthur focused on liquor, banking, real estate, and entertainment, Jimmy concentrated on sports. At first, that meant the Blackhawks and Red Wings, but as the 1940s dawned, Jimmy plunged headlong into a new venture that he rightly believed held vastly more promise for riches than the anemic NHL.

Boxing, known back then as prize fighting, held the nation in its clutches the way football would later grunt and shove its way to the top of the professional sports landscape. A major heavyweight championship fight back then could command weeks of front-page coverage and pack seventy-thousand-seat stadiums. Bolstering the sport was a newfangled appliance known as a television, which, despite its fuzzy black-and-white images and the fickleness of rabbit-ear antennae, was swiftly becoming as essential to a man's possessions as a pair of slippers and a newspaper by the chair. While TV would have struggled back then to present sports played on bigger fields, it was uniquely suited to capture the drama going on in the small square of a boxing ring. As usual, Arthur perceived the possibilities immediately and, by dint of owning many of the country's big arenas, turned the technology to his and Norris's advantage.

Consolidating their hold, Jimmy and Arthur formed the International Boxing Club in 1949, creating a prepackaged supply of boxing shows for the increasingly popular Wednesday and Friday night fights on TV. Leveraging their arena ownership, including Chicago Stadium and, most lucratively, Madison Square Garden, they controlled who fought whom and when, who was a contender, and who was fated to struggle in anonymity.

Fittingly, in a rough-and-tumble game that included characters as dangerous as they were colorful—mobsters, swindlers, and grifters of all types—Jimmy served as the public face of the partnership. Arthur contented himself as the "inside man"—the guy with the money.

No matter who was out front, the partners threw haymakers. If a contender, or a contender's promoter, wanted to land a big fight, for instance, he either kissed Jimmy and Arthur's ring or roamed the darker and bloodier world of club fights paid in drinks and perhaps a sliver of the night's door receipts.

At boxing's peak, from 1949 to 1955, the Wirtz- and Norris-owned IBC promoted forty-seven out of fifty-one championship bouts held in the United States. The four they missed were minor fights that the IBC—and the public—couldn't have cared less about.

Dominating the market is one thing, a monopoly is another—and unfair practices including collusion and fight fixing to create a stranglehold another still. With the IBC, allegations of boxers taking dives to advance the careers of the favored and to line the pockets of the unsavory blossomed as commonly as welts under the eyes of hapless pugs. Wirtz and Norris "run everything in boxing," Jack (Doc) Kearns, manager of Archie Moore, once complained. "And when they feel like it, they throw you a bone." As for collusion, promoters knew that crossing the IBC spelled career doom—for them and their fighters.

Jimmy and Arthur's iron-fisted rule, coupled with the shady characters leeching off the sport—the mobster "Hoodlum Frankie Carbo" chief among them—eventually drew the attention of federal investigators. Neither Jimmy, who was close friends with Carbo, nor Arthur was much worried—yet. They were too busy enjoying the creature comforts that were the spoils of the vast stores of wealth and power they were amassing. King Arthur, for example, was consumed with the construction of his Camelot, an elegant country redoubt built on the bones of the family farm in Fremont settled so long ago by the original American Wirtz, Michael.

A simple working concern back then, the property had been transformed into Ivanhoe, an oasis with all the charms and appurtenances of a gentleman's countryside estate. Ranging over four hundred acres, Ivanhoe offered riding stables, a majestic outdoor fountain, and Arthur's favorite feature—a twelve-foot deep, kidney-shaped pool straddled on either side by glassed-in changing houses complete with bars and locker rooms as handsomely outfitted as any country club's.

The elegantly appointed main house featured a dining room that, while perhaps not a challenge to the Hall of Mirrors at Versailles, drew gasps nonetheless from visitors. Chandeliers draped from the ceiling. China cabinets and hutch dressers brimmed with priceless dishes culled from trips overseas, antiques, and heirlooms. The shelves tinkled with cut lead crystal goblets and fine stemware, and drawers gleamed with six-piece, sterling silver, Wallace Silversmiths settings. Virginia put the elegant tableware to regular use at Sunday dinners and any time the couple was entertaining friends and clients.

The paneled basement featured a long bar stocked with liquors from the Wirtz company and watched over by an oil painting of Sonja

Henie that included an inscription, "to Arthur and Queenie, love, Sonja." The centerpiece of the room—at the time—was something of a marvel in an era before DVRs and premium cable channels: a drop-down movie screen where guests could watch first-run films. The man in charge of technical gadgetry at Chicago Stadium ran the projector.

For moments of repose, there was the library—bright, redolent of the leather-bound books lining its custom shelves—its giant picture windows affording a view onto grass as closely shaved as a golf fairway. And, finally, there were the six upstairs bedrooms, including the master suite to which Arthur and Virginia retired after an evening's entertainment. Rocky recalls being summoned to the room to find Arthur, Churchillian in silk pajamas and puffing a Cuban cigar—to fetch letters his grandfather wanted conveyed to the town post office.

Virginia enjoyed perks of her own—namely, a black Rolls Royce Silver Cloud that ferried her around town in queenly splendor. Parked regally out front and most often piloted by an English chauffeur imported by Arthur for the purpose, the vehicle transported the lady of the manor to and fro in the city, and even to Blackhawks games (where she was, to the delight of Arthur and fans, a fan as zealous as any 300-level devotee).

But in what was another of her endearing eccentricities, she also liked to climb behind the wheel herself. And so, on Wednesdays in the summer, Virginia could be seen tootling up the Edens, an exotic bonnet perched on her head and white gloves protecting her manicured hands, en route to Ivanhoe to prepare for the weekend arrival of children and grandchildren from the city. Yet again, however, she defied easy description. Her mode of transport may have been extravagant, but the thought of paying a thirty-cent toll so nettled her that she would wind an extra hour on back roads to reach her destination.

On those summer days in the country, the grandchildren, including Rocky, would grime themselves shoveling out the stables and pigpens. By night, freshly showered and neatly dressed, they pulled up to a table set for royalty—with assorted silver salad, dessert, and dinner forks, demitasses, and fine china and fresh flowers in cut-crystal vases. Diners dipped their hands in finger bowls and dabbed the corners of their mouths with freshly laundered linen napkins. Waiters in starched white coats, silent as monks, glided in and out of the kitchen to clear plates, replenish wine glasses, and ferry the next course. If any of the children snickered at the formality, they did not do so in front of their grandmother and she made no apologies for her insistence on what others might have seen as frivolous custom. For they knew, as did Arthur, what lay behind her fondness for elegance: her parents, before the Depression took all, had laid just such a table.

If Virginia had her Rolls and expensive China, Arthur had his own somewhat extravagant indulgence. In the late 1960s and early 1970s, he began commissioning the building of first one yacht, then a larger one, then a larger one still. He christened each the *Blackhawk*, attaching successive Roman numerals, and docked them in Coral Gables, Florida, where he often met Jimmy for fishing trips in Biscayne Bay and, occasionally, the deeper seas of the Bermuda Triangle. Family photos show Arthur, in shirt sleeves and captain's hat, piloting the yachts out to hunt marlin and other big game fish.

The yachts also scratched what was for Arthur a lifelong itch. "He loved building and designing things," says Rocky, who inherited the penchant. With *Yacht Blackhawk*, for instance—a 123-foot-long Dutch Feadship—Arthur personally traveled to the Netherlands in the late 1960s to oversee its construction. He even contributed to the design of its hull and other features, including a desalter that could change forty gallons of seawater into freshwater to meet the demands of the craft's three baths (with showers), four master staterooms, and crew's quarters, as well as the on-board washing machines. Forever sensitive to the heat, he also made sure each room had its own air-conditioning.

Had it not been for the famously unpredictable weather in the fall, Arthur might have taken the helm and crossed the Atlantic himself. Instead, in a marvel of engineering at the time, the *Yacht Blackhawk* was loaded into the hull of an even bigger ship for the trip to Coral Gables. (In an interesting coincidence, Arthur and Virginia had planned to cruise in the Mediterranean earlier in the summer, but construction of the original yacht was delayed by three months when much of its equipment went down with the freighter *Finland*, which burned and sank near Havre, France, the very port from which Michael disembarked for America nearly 101 years earlier to the month.)

On a more practical level, Arthur, like his father, Fred, made sure that his children attended the best private schools. He enrolled Bill, for example, in Chicago's Latin School for Boys (now the Latin School of Chicago). Founded at the end of the nineteenth century by a group of parents concerned about the state of education in the city, the brown-brick Latin school rose in the heart of the city's fabled Gold Coast and quickly became the school of choice for Chicago's moneyed class. A natural athlete, Bill starred in football and track and a sport perfectly suited for the pugnacious young man: boxing. He also earned the kinds of grades necessary to gain entry into an Ivy League school and indeed, when it came time to choose a college, he opted for Brown University, in Providence, Rhode Island.

His time there was uneventful save for one raucous incident—telling in retrospect—that occurred when he was out with his fellow Brown Bears at a local bar. Family lore holds that Bill was having a fine time, downing pitchers of beer and regaling the boys with one story after another, when a compact, dark-haired, and thickly muscled young man accidentally spilled a beer on him. Wheeling in fury, Bill recognized the offender. It was a boxer named Rocco Marchegiano. Having boxed himself, Bill not only wasn't intimidated, he was eager to settle the score, which he did by dumping a pitcher on the boxer's head. Marchegiano promptly decked Bill. A brawl ensued. Police broke up the scuffle and tossed the offenders into a cell to let them sleep it off. Bill got the worst of it, including a fat shiner and a concussion. Terrified of contacting Arthur to bail him out, however, Bill instead used his phone call to contact a rescuer he rightly assumed would be more sympathetic to his plight, Jimmy Norris. Bill cooled his heels for two days in the Providence lockup, the time it took Jimmy to arrive. After he was sprung, Bill—as the story goes—said, "Jimmy, this guy can punch." About few things had Bill ever been as prophetic. The young man—who not long after adopted the name Rocky Marciano—went on to become one of the greatest boxers in history—and a friend of Bill's for life.

Fathers and Sons

As evidenced by snapshots taken in the years immediately following his graduation from Brown, the Bill Wirtz of the 1950s and 1960s was far from the caricature he would become later in life: the chain-smoker with the porcine face and fleshy nose. Nor was he the vindictive crank he was at the end—a bitter, sad figure whose grudges splintered his family and put the crown jewel of the dynasty, the Blackhawks, into a perilous financial position.

Rather, the Bill Wirtz of those halcyon years strode the halls of Wirtz Corp. as a rakish, sharp-eyed, smooth talker with a dry wit, a seemingly bottomless well of stories, and a shrewd head for business. "Women looked at Bill like he was a movie star," recalls Bruce Wirtz MacArthur. Photos indeed reveal a vigorous, model-handsome go-getter ready to assume control of the family business when Arthur deemed him ready. (Model handsome is not an exaggeration. After Bill took the helm of the Blackhawks in 1966, Old Fitzgerald bourbon featured him in a print ad, posed in a blue blazer and yachting cap tipped, cradling a drink in his hand. The copy reads, "Success. How to handle it.")

As Arthur's oldest son, Bill's ascension to the head of Wirtz Corp. was assured. Arthur held to the principle—later codified in a binding succession plan—that the eldest Wirtz male would assume control of the family business through at least three generations. Under the arrangement, that meant Bill's brother,

Arthur Michael Wirtz Jr.—Michael—was next in line, following Bill.

Even so, Bill hesitated when it came time to join the family business. At Brown, he majored in the classics and for a time considered traveling overseas for an archeological dig. More intriguing still was a little-known offer he received from one of the deans at Brown. At the time, the Central Intelligence Agency preferred to hunt its recruits at Ivy League schools. According to Rocky, some of the deans were charged with scouting promising prospects. Bill landed on their radar as a bright, dynamic natural leader. "They called him in like you'd see in a movie and said, 'I'm not really John Brown. I'm so-and-so, head of recruiting for the CIA,'" Rocky explains, "'and we want you to join.' They wanted him to be a spy and work in the Intelligence division but he turned them down."

Instead, Bill spent the next three years working as a certified public accountant with a firm outside the Wirtz family business. He would join Arthur soon enough, but at the time, his priority was establishing a family of his own. "He wanted to get married and settle down," Rocky says.

The object of his affections was a shy, dark-haired young woman named Joan Louise Roney. Pretty, her hair styled into a Sandy Dennis bob, and with eyes the color of a fine bourbon held in front of a light, Joan was far less self-assured than her brash Ivy League suitor with the flashing eyes and confident swagger. She possessed a quick wit and a wry sense of humor, however, that allowed her to give as good as she got, and a personality warmed by a sunny outlook—qualities that appealed to Bill deeply. She could hardly be called vain, but one thing made her self-conscious: she was a year older than Bill. (The difference bothered her so much that when she died years later, Bill shaved a year off her age on her tombstone.)

Different as they were, the strengths of Bill and Joan complemented each other just as they did with Arthur and Virginia. Arthur was the empire builder; Virginia held the social connections. Bill liked a good time, but was given to brooding and frightening flashes of anger. Joan had a way of both protecting him and keeping his ego in check. "He would tell a story and she would say, 'Now, Billy Wirtz, that isn't true,'" recalls Rocky. "And he would take it."

The two liked highballs and socializing, Bill perhaps a little more than the slightly introverted Joan. As for sports, well, Bill actually loved the Blackhawks as well as ran them. Unlike Virginia, however, Joan was nothing like a super fan. She liked seeing the team do well because it made Bill happy—certainly less prone to grouchiness—and she went to her share of games. But in private moments she confessed she much preferred staying home to venturing into the beer-and-brat stadium for a three-hour tilt. But she also didn't begrudge Bill his proclivities, including dining late into the evenings with Jimmy Norris.

What Bill and Joan shared most—and what cemented their compatibility—were the circumstances in which each had been brought up. Both families had Illinois farm roots dating to the 1800s—the Wirtz's Ivanhoe farm in Fremont, the Roney's estate just down the road in Wauconda. In both families, a relative broke away from the farm to seek his fortune in the big city. By the time of Bill's courtship of Joan, both the Wirtzes and the Roneys circulated in Chicago's rarified social circles. The Roney's wealth derived from a chain of fifty-four High-Low grocery stores, a business founded in 1938 by Joan's father, Walter. Joan's mother, Katherine Rockwell, was a thirteenth-generation descendant of Samuel Fuller, who came to America on the Mayflower.

In a charming gesture his later detractors might find surprising, Bill courted his fiancée on horseback. On spring and summer weekends, he would saddle up at the family farm and ride the five or so miles to the Roney place in Wauconda, where Joan, an accomplished equestrian in her own right, waited with her horse. Together, they would ride the countryside between the two homesteads.

Out of deference to Joan's Roman Catholic faith, the couple exchanged their vows on December 16, 1950, at St. Philip Neri Catholic Church on the South Side. Afterward, they boarded a jet for a honeymoon in Mexico. Things got off to a tough start when Bill contracted typhoid fever and an intestinal bug of some kind, but the setback, far from an omen of bad things to come, merely entered family lore as a comical side note to a lasting and durable relationship.

Two years later, in a coincidence that defies mathematical probability, Joan gave birth to a son on Bill's birthday, October 5, 1952.

The couple named him William Rockwell Wirtz, the middle name in honor of his maternal grandmother, Katherine Rockwell, and William after his dad. From the start, however, he was known simply as Rocky. As it happened, Bill's boxer buddy, Rocky Marciano, assumed the parents had named the boy after him. "When I was born, he sent my mother a flower arrangement with little boxing gloves," Rocky says. Bill didn't have the heart to set the record straight—not with Marciano, at least—and the boxer would cling to the misunderstanding for the rest of his life. Either way, the nickname not only stuck. It fit.

In the following years, the couple added four more children to the family. Gail followed Rocky by a year and a half. Karey came next, then Peter in 1959, and finally, Alison.

The joy of Rocky's birth was tempered by a sad development just two months later. James E. "Pop" Norris, age seventy-four, collapsed from a heart attack and died. While he had "business interests scattered all over the world," the *Chicago Tribune* noted, he was best known as the promoter and owner of hockey teams and for his partnership with Arthur. During his long rivalry with then Blackhawks owner Major McLaughlin, the obituary said, "nothing pleased [Norris] more than a victory of his Red Wings over the Black Hawks."

Fortunately, the disposition of the patriarch's assets was a smooth one. By the time of his death, Pop Norris had already ceded his interest in Chicago Stadium and the Blackhawks to his two sons, Jimmy and Jimmy's half-brother, Bruce, and to his lifelong pal and partner, Arthur.

Jimmy remained a vice president with the Red Wings. (He named his sister Marguerite president, making her the first woman to head an NHL franchise. She held the position for three years, before giving way to her brother, Bruce.) But Jimmy turned his energies to the long-neglected Blackhawks, sharing day-to-day operations with Arthur.

When Bill finally joined the family company in 1954, Arthur steered him toward the real estate and eventually the liquor holdings. Like Arthur, he became fast friends with Jimmy Norris. The two, in fact, would soon become drinking buddies as well as business associates, shutting down the Pump Room, the celebrity restaurant in the

Ambassador East Hotel. "Bill loved him," says Bruce Wirtz MacArthur. "He loved to tell Jimmy Norris stories." Rocky likewise adored the colorful Norris, irrepressible even into his fifties. "We called him Uncle Jimmy," says Rocky. "He was this Playboy type. Good looking. He had an apartment here, but he'd hop down to his home in Florida, Coral Gables, or up to New York, where we had an office."

At the time, however, Jimmy Norris and Arthur—not Jimmy and Bill—were the ones spending most of their time together and not in a pleasant way. The feds, having had the partners in their crosshairs for years, now pounced. Concerned over what they saw as the IBC's stranglehold over boxing—and worse, the organization's cozy relationship with the "clique of hoodlums, racketeers and surething gamblers" who were part of that world (as charged in a 1952 *Life* magazine article)—federal trustbusters wanted to shut the IBC down.

In a withering exposé that took apart Norris, New York Athletic Commissioner Robert K. Christenberry argued that the sport faced "the gravest crisis in its history," a moment of truth that demanded a reckoning. "It is already a matter of record that crooks have fixed fights in the course of pulling off betting coups," Christenberry wrote. "More importantly, they have muscled in on fighters, managers, and promoters to fleece them of their earnings. They have punished some who have resisted by making it difficult or impossible for them to get matches, while rewarding their captives with strings of reputation-building victories over pushovers."

The undisputed face of the growing scandal, Christenberry charged, was the IBC's "multimillionaire president, James D. Norris Jr."—Jimmy. Arthur Wirtz's name never appears in the *Life* article. But as "the inside man—the money guy," as Rocky puts it, Arthur was deeply involved.

To his credit, he warned his partner off of his mob associations. "Arthur would tell [Jimmy] 'You can't do that. Your reputation is everything,'" Rocky says.

The same year the New York Athletic Commission went after the IBC, the federal government sued the group under the Sherman Antitrust Act. The allegations included charges that Jimmy and Arthur, through "tight, brutal control," fixed bouts, managed boxers off the books, consorted with mob figures, and used intimidation to force boxers to hire their associates as advisors. Both Norris and Wirtz were named as defendants.

The IBC case, meanwhile, bounced around the courts for years—twice to the U.S. Supreme Court, where the justices decided that baseball's exemption from the antitrust laws didn't apply to boxing. The government ultimately won and broke the IBC's iron grip on the sport. In 1959, Norris and Wirtz dissolved their interest in the organization. A year later, Norris was hauled before Congress to testify about his role in the scandal. Now fifty-four, he was no longer the cocksure man about town. Instead, "wearing a somber tan and a funeral suit . . . he walked with the reluctant step of a man approaching the gallows," *Sports Illustrated* reported. "Indeed, the jig was up."

Norris testified that he had indeed been associated, both personally and professionally, with the mobster Frankie Carbo, who was sentenced to twenty-five years in prison for conspiracy and extortion. Because Arthur had remained in the background, he "escaped most of the serious repercussions that went with the revelations of criminal ties," the *Wall Street Journal* wrote, quoting a lawyer representing the IBC. "Arthur never got involved with those guys [gangsters] because he left the promotion end to Jim. Of course, if it wasn't for Arthur," the attorney, Truman Gibson, added, "we never would have got to the point where the government had to break us up."

Despite the scandal, Arthur and Jimmy emerged relatively unscathed. Indeed, they found a way to come out ahead, selling their stock in Madison Square Garden for $4 million, widely considered more than they had paid for the arena, "and realized another hefty profit from their later disposal of the St. Louis Arena," according to the *Journal.*

• • •

By then, though, the fortunes of the Blackhawks had changed for the better—by an order of magnitude. It had been a long haul to lift the franchise from its sorry state in 1945, when Pop Norris and Arthur had acquired the team. That 1944–45 season, the Hawks won a paltry thirteen games and the team made the playoffs just twice in the next thirteen years. But after Pop died in 1952, and Jimmy took a stronger interest in the Hawks, the team staged a turnaround. With Arthur as president, he lured Tommy Ivan, general manager of the rival Detroit Red Wings, to take over the Chicago franchise. Ivan's track record spoke for itself. His teams had won three Stanley Cups—in 1950, 1952, and 1954—and six straight regular-season NHL championships. His first move was to build the Hawks' nonexistent farm system. Then, persuading Arthur to open his wallet, he bought two talent-stocked minor league clubs. (The teams included two future hockey Hall of Famers: Bobby Hull and Pierre Pilote.)

In 1961, two years after the dissolution of the IBC, Jimmy enjoyed a last big hurrah. The substantial investments in the hockey team's farm club and other savvy moves had stocked the team with a group of all-stars, many of whom would wind up in the Hall of Fame. Four years earlier, for example, general manager Ivan took advantage of a fit of pique by his counterpart in Detroit against the young goalie sensation, Glenn Hall. In his first year with the Red Wings, Hall earned rookie of the year honors. The second year, he won the Vezina trophy, awarded to the goaltender who allowed the fewest goals during the regular season. He did not lead Detroit to a Stanley Cup championship, however, and so general manager Jack Adams traded him to the Blackhawks. Hall would go on to be a ten-time all-star, three-time Vezina winner, and win the Conn Smythe Trophy for the most valuable player in the postseason. The Hawks also had Pilote and the man who is now widely regarded as one of the best ever: Bobby Hull, the "Golden Jet." Added to a roster that included Stan Mikita, another future Hall of Famer, and a list of solid role players, the 1961 Hawks skated into the playoffs as the franchise's best hope for a Stanley Cup in more than two decades.

The road to the championship, however, led through a seemingly impenetrable wall: the Montreal Canadiens. The Canadiens had been in the finals a staggering ten years in a row. In 1961, they were gunning to capture the league's Holy Grail for a record sixth straight time. In the semifinals, however, the Hawks upset the Canadiens in six games, creating a matchup with a fitting nemesis in the finals: the Detroit Red Wings.

With the help of co-owner Jimmy Norris, Arthur, as team president, had managed to pull off the seemingly impossible—bringing the Blackhawks from last-place laughingstock four years before to the brink of glory. At that time, Bill had not yet joined the team, but Michael, his younger brother by five years, was already a vice president.

One of the team's biggest and most unlikely fans was Virginia, who "never missed a game," according to the papers. As was fitting with someone of her breeding, she wore large bonnets to the game and sat behind the Blackhawks bench, where she feigned obliviousness to the profanity raining down from the well-lubricated fans around her. To memorialize her devotion, she proudly pinned a custom-made brooch—a ticket stub fashioned out of gold and encrusted with jewels bearing her seat number—to her blouse.

Rocky, nine years old at the time, rooted for the team, of course, but he would not begin attending games for another year and thus missed out on the excitement that held the entire city in its grip.

The team won the first game against Detroit 3–2, behind two goals by Hull, including the game winner. Detroit bounced back to win the second game, 3–1, but the Hawks returned the favor in game three, winning by the same 3–1 score. After trading wins in games four and five, the Hawks blew Detroit out in game six, 5–1, hoisting the Cup for the first time since 1938. Today, Arthur's Round Table boardroom features a framed photo of him and Norris grinning beside the trophy.

Given the youth of the team, and its powerhouse lineup of talent, it seemed at the time that it might be the first of many. As fate would have it, however, the Blackhawks would not win another championship for forty-nine years—and only then after the arrival of the most unlikely of deliverers, a new owner with no experience running a professional sports franchise and a team in such desperate straits that much of the city had abandoned hopes that it could ever break away.

The Son Also Rises

He was thirteen years old—a well-mannered sixth grader with a sly glint nonetheless, who liked sports and his habitual group of friends at North Shore Country Day School—when his father sat him down for a talk about what his boy would be doing for the rest of his life.

Father and son sat in the living room of the family's Winnetka, Illinois, house, a sprawling, two-story white colonial, with black-shuttered windows lining the front and a towering chimney competing for dominance with the surrounding trees, its somewhat charmless facade not unlike a well-kept motel for guests at a suburban corporate HQ. Bill had moved the family there when Rocky was four, and within a few years, the family, now numbering a total of five children, quickly established itself as a fixture of the moneyed enclave.

In accordance with family custom, Rocky dressed rather formally for a teenager in the 1960s. His friends favored tie-dye and jeans. Rocky, almost without exception, sported pleated khakis, polished shoes, an ironed dress shirt, and a navy sports jacket. He wore his thick hair carefully combed and cleaved into a neat left-to-right part.

"We used to kid Rocky about his Rocky stay-press pants and his stay-press hair," says a childhood friend, Bob Jordan, with whom Rocky is still close.

"Perma-hair," Rocky calls it. "Take the football helmet off and it would look the same. They could never quite understand it. 'How does your hair stay the same?' I don't know."

Far from shunning their clean-cut friend, whom they grew to realize wasn't the "square" they thought, they capitalized on his appearance. "The great thing about having Rocky around was that you could take him home to your parents and they all loved him," says Jordan. "We could be going out for all kinds of mischief, but if Rocky was along we could get away with it."

Realizing the ribbing was good natured, Rocky came to relish his role in the group. Not that it would have mattered if Rocky had wanted to loosen up his look. The dress code was an unspoken rule in the Wirtz household, and, as would be the case during his forty-one-year reign as Blackhawks president, Bill would not countenance anything approaching disobedience. If Rocky's friends—or students at school—gave him a hard time, tough. No son of his was going to dress like a hippie.

In this meeting, as was typical at home and work, Bill's tone brooked no foolishness. Accordingly, he got right to the point. A few months earlier in that year, 1965, Rocky's grandpa Arthur had laid out the terms of family succession, Bill explained, executing a binding plan. When his grandfather died, Bill, as the oldest son, would take over the family business. Similarly, Bill said, when he, Bill, died, his younger brother Michael would assume command. After that, him. Rocky.

Understood?

The sixth grader nodded.

Another thirteen-year-old might have been taken aback. Bill was, in effect, deciding his son's life path for him, a path that would eventually lead to his being responsible for the company upon which the entire family, not to mention thousands of employees and the Wirtz name itself, depended. He would do so without question, at the expense of his own dreams—if he dared dream them—or any other frivolous notions a young man his age might have entertained.

Rocky, however, received the information with aplomb—a reaction that would have surprised exactly no one who knew him well. From the start, the young heir displayed a maturity and sense of responsibility beyond his years. In a way, he had to. As the oldest of his parents' five children, his father worked twelve- to fourteen-hour days in the family's liquor and real estate businesses. Within a year Bill would add the presidency of the Blackhawks to his already-staggering load. Their mother stayed home and was a guiding figure, to be sure. But in his father's absence, Rocky, as outdated as the term may be today, was the man of the house. It was a role that came naturally to him. As dutiful as he could be—and was, at least early on—he was also strong willed. Those who knew him, in fact, recognized flashes of his famously imposing grandfather, Arthur. He would keep his mouth shut, but only to a point. When that line was crossed, he would stand up for himself with anyone, including his father, Bill.

"I was the only one in the family who would stand up to Dad," Rocky says. "Which was understandable, because he was tough." Indeed, the fallout for such audacity could be dire—an explosion from Bill or, equally as punishing, silence that could last for weeks. Painful as such repercussions were, Rocky refused to retreat. "I was not going to back down."

Rocky's headstrong character almost certainly owed in part to his father. Growing up, Rocky never doubted Bill's devotion. His dad attended most all of his sporting events and, along with his mother, welcomed Rocky's friends into the home. But Bill was also stern, dictatorial, and on occasion downright mean. On Rocky's tenth birthday, for example, Bill had promised to take his son and a group of friends for a party and an ice show at Chicago Stadium. "I was misbehaving in some way," Rocky told *Chicago* magazine many years later. "Before we left, he said, 'If you do that again, I'm leaving you behind.' Naturally I tested him. Sure enough, the family station wagon went right down to Chicago Stadium with all my friends, and I got left home." Although Rocky shares the tale with an utter lack of self-pity, the notion of a father abandoning his boy over a silly infraction—on his birthday, no less—and *taking his friends on to the celebration without him* is the kind of scarring stuff that allows shrinks to pay for their own kids' braces. For Rocky, there was little else to do but take it in stride. "It's just the way Dad was," he says.

At the same time, Bill was clearly grooming his son. Rocky recalls a lot of "vacations" in which Bill would mix work and pleasure—say, a liquor convention. "So I'd get exposure to these folks in the business." Or Bill would take an overnight trip out West "because we had a liquor house in San Francisco," says Rocky. "I'd fly out with him and we'd come right back, but I'd get to meet some of the executives." The truth is, "I was attracted to it."

At home, Rocky's adult-like demeanor didn't always go over well with his siblings—Gail, Karey, Peter, and Alison—who at times found him acting more like a parent than their peer. That was fine. Resentment came with the territory. "We got along," Rocky says. "The thing is, when you're the oldest of five, you have to kind of set the stage for the other four. But, yes, the idea that one day Dad wasn't going to be around and big brother was going to take over was tough on them."

There were few perks that came with the job of big brother, but one of them was a bona fide gift. When Rocky reached driving age, he inherited the family's wood-paneled station wagon. The vehicle made for a homely chariot for a teenager looking to land dates (Bill, who drove a black Cadillac, refused to buy something more stylish) but Rocky loved it: "You could fit nine people in that thing," he recalls. "So you'd pile all your buddies in and you'd cruise around." And they did. To drive-ins, to burger joints, and occasionally the big city to take in the sights.

During summers, Rocky earned his spending money at the family farm, shoveling manure and baling hay with the hired hands under the broiling sun. "Hogs and horses," Rocky recalls. "From eight to ten thirty you cleaned up after the hogs, then you'd spread the manure so that by eleven o'clock you started doing some field work. Mow hay. Rake it. Bale it." To this day, a long, creosote, split rail fence that Rocky built runs the length of the Ivanhoe farm entrance. "I would work there Monday through Friday and get paid X amount of dollars, then come home for the weekends. That would last until August, when I'd start football practice."

If his supervisory treatment of his siblings didn't always go over well, Rocky's one-of-the-guys ethos earned him a group of loyal friends, some of whom he still counts as close. Bob Jordan, for instance, met Rocky while the two attended North Shore Country Day. "If anybody was expected to be Richie Rich, born with the silver spoon stereotype, it was Rocky," says Jordan, who today lives in Bozeman, Montana. "In fact, he went out of his way not to be snooty or arrogant."

"I look back at some of the pictures in our yearbook," agrees another close friend, Walter Goldstein, "and there's Rocky, pretty much everywhere that we were. We'd all go off in his station wagon, driving around town. He had a great way of getting along with everybody."

Rocky credits the school, which he attended from kindergarten through high school, for his ability later in life to do what neither Arthur nor Bill ever could: stay on friendly terms with virtually anybody. At North Shore, "even those who were a little odd, let's say, you'd get along with those folks," Rocky says. "They couldn't fit into a large public high school. They would really have been bullied or denigrated, so they went to North Shore for a little more attention and a little more collegial atmosphere."

• • •

The normalcy Bill and Joan sought for their kids did not mean that the family lived below its means. There was the somewhat grand home, to which Bill added a family room, a second master bedroom, and a pool.

The Wirtzes took vacations, sent their children to excellent private schools, dined at the city's best restaurants, and enjoyed the amenities of the Wirtz-owned Bismarck Hotel (where Bill took Rocky to get his monthly haircut from his own clip guy, Bert the Barber). Summers offered a favorite pastime for Joan and later her daughters—riding horses at Ivanhoe and competing in regional equestrian events. And then there were the fringe benefits of having a father who ran one of the city's sports franchises—private parties for the kids at Chicago Stadium, regular downtown junkets to see the Blackhawks play.

The closeness of the family in those days is captured in a portrait of the entire clan gathered together on the stairs of the family home. Had it been a publicity still for *The Brady Bunch*, the fictional family from the 1960s sitcom, the photograph of the Wirtzes—Bill, Joan, Rocky, Gail, Peter, Alison, and Karey—could not have been more wholesome. All neatly dressed—blazers for the men and boys, skirts for the women and girls, a wide-lapeled suit for Joan—they beamed for the camera, a happy image all the more poignant given the obliviousness to the fraught drama that lay in the future.

Back then, Bill still had a short fuse, but he also showed a more jovial, social side, even with Rocky's friends. "The Wirtz household was kind of the social center," recalls Jordan. "Everybody knew each other, so on Friday and Saturday nights it wasn't unusual to have five or six people hanging out there."

Rocky's pals would sometimes see Bill come in late in the evening—"always dressed very nattily," Goldstein recalls. "Great suit, great appearance. We didn't really think much about him running the Blackhawks. It's just the way it was."

Occasionally, Bill and Joan would come downstairs and join the party—Joan tossing zingers at Rocky's friends and Bill sharing insider tales of the city's hockey team. "Bill would put a robe on, and we'd all hang around the kitchen and everybody's drinking margaritas or daiquiris or something and we'd have a ball with them," recalls John Miller, another lifelong friend who went on to become president of North American Corp. of Illinois.

Wirtz Family Values

The organ had barely faded and the last echo of the eulogy for Jimmy Norris had hardly died out when Arthur named Bill president of the Blackhawks and Michael senior vice president. At Arthur's direction, Bill would also join the NHL Board of Governors—a seeming formality that in short order would have major consequences for that body, the league, and the game itself.

The team moved on swiftly too. Having paid their respects to Norris the night of his death, February 25, 1966, the players flew to Detroit for a game against the Red Wings, a team whose new president was Jimmy Norris's sister, Marguerite Ann. Her ascendancy, included in Jimmy's will, made her the first female team executive in NHL history. She shared ownership of the club with Jimmy's half-brother, Bruce Norris.

In that game, much more was at stake for the Hawks than wanting to make a good showing against the Norris-owned team. The Blackhawks needed a win to maintain its first place tie with Montreal, and Bobby Hull was chasing the NHL scoring record—which he already shared—of fifty goals in a season.

After a crowd of 14,560 in Olympia Arena observed a moment of silence for Jimmy Norris, the Hawks came through on both counts. The team notched a 4–1 victory, while Hull netted his forty-eighth goal, the game winner, the latter adding yet more evidence that in him, Chicago had the best player in the league and perhaps one of the best ever, the Michael Jordan of his day. What was not known at the time was how ugly that glorious story would turn, and the lasting damage it would do to not just Rocky's father, but the Wirtz name. For few athletes before or since have inflamed the passions of a city, a league, a sport, and a nation the way Robert Marvin Hull did when he burst onto the scene as a full-time player for the Blackhawks in 1957.

With blazing speed and power (at his peak, he could skate nearly thirty miles per hour), and a slap shot once clocked at 118.3 miles per hour, the left winger led the league in both goals and points by his third season. His on-ice prowess—coupled with his brassy cap of golden blond hair, gleaming white smile, and charismatic swagger—fit perfectly with his nickname: the Golden Jet. Rocky recalls being awestruck when he met the superstar. "I'd never seen arms that big on a person," Rocky says. "I kept saying to myself, 'How could he fit his arms in a regular golf shirt?' You know, today you see body builders, but back then you didn't see that stuff. No steroids, just from working on the farm."

That spring of 1966, Hull went on to break the seventy-game season record by scoring fifty-four goals and totaling ninety-seven points, another NHL record. Behind the play of Hull and the team's other stars—Mikita and Pilote—the Hawks went to the playoffs, but lost in the semifinals to the Red Wings in six games. The Hawks made the postseason again the next two years, including in 1967–68, the season the league expanded to twelve teams in two divisions.

The Bill Wirtz era as the head of the Blackhawks was off to a reasonably promising start. Then came the 1968–69 season. Despite a scoring barrage from Hull that would end with a new record of fifty-eight goals, the Hawks plummeted to a spot all too familiar to pre–Bill Wirtz fans: the cellar.

Bill Wirtz had a way of dealing with underperforming assets. On March 1, 1969, with nearly a month left in the season, he burst into a tirade for the ages to a reporter for the *Chicago Tribune.* The headline screamed from the newspaper's front page: "Bill Wirtz Vows 'Sweeping Changes' for the Hawks." Shocking for its threats, its dark tone, and the rage that singed nearly every quote, the article featured a professional team president doing what such bosses almost never did: ripping the players. He questioned their heart, sneered at their injuries, and condemned them with the worst word you can call a professional athlete: soft. Other than Hull, whom he praised, no one escaped his wrath, including himself.

"My father put me in charge of this club," Bill fumed in the article's opening sentence, "and I may be fired. But I wouldn't be the only one to change uniforms."

Forty years old at the time, Bill railed against what he perceived as the lack of an "honest effort" by the players. "It isn't the losing that irritates me, it's the way they lose; the lack of desire," he said. "I don't go for the injuries excuse. Professional athletes worthy of the big league name should have enough pride in themselves to come up in emergencies, play better than they know how, extend themselves to take up the slack. Winners rise up in the clutch and win the games they must win."

Wirtz professed confidence in coach Billy Reay, general manager Tommy Ivan, and Hull, but issued an ominous warning to everyone else: at the end of the season, Wirtz said, "we will reappraise every player on the club. . . . We will not protect anyone." The days of "coddling and pampering" were over.

Bill's words were every bit as charged as they sounded. The reporter, Ted Damata, characterized him as "angry, crackling," when he spoke. Damata concluded with an anecdote suggesting that Arthur shared his son's fury. "It was late, after the Hawks had lost another bad one in the stadium," Damata wrote. "Huddled in the darkened concourse were Mr. and Mrs. [Arthur] Wirtz and their two sons, William and Michael." Arthur beckoned the reporter. "Don't you want to know what I think of the team?" Arthur growled. "I'll tell you. Tomorrow morning I'm taking a plane to Florida where I can work unperturbed and where the air is uncontaminated!"

The harangue by Bill and additional derision by Arthur flabbergasted not only the NHL (the article would be referenced at a Board of Governor's meeting later in the spring), but the fans, the players, the coaches, and the front office—almost everyone, in fact, except people like Rocky, for whom such outbursts were all too familiar.

• • •

Rocky, sixteen at the time, had more important things on his mind than an outburst from his dad—namely, where to go to college in a couple of years. As with most things in his life involving his future, he already had given the matter much thought and come up with a rough outline of wheres and whens. He wasn't sure exactly where he would land, but he knew it would be far away from Bill, from his siblings, from front-page rants and the daily reminders of the weight he would one day bear.

He wouldn't stay away for long. Two years at most, then back home to finish up at a school that had danced in his imagination since he was ten and for which he had stood on the sidewalk to watch its homecoming parade.

That evening, the Northwestern University Wildcat band marched by in their purple and white, followed by a caravan of sashed beauty queens waving from convertibles and decorated floats. "There was just something very exciting about it," he recalls. "I didn't care what it took, I was going to go there at some point."

In doing so, he would be following in the footsteps of both Virginia and his Aunt Betty, who had loved the experience so much that they would in time donate huge sums to their alma mater.

First, however, he looked to the East. "I knew I wanted to be somewhere that had a good hockey program," he recalls. Not to play—football and boxing had been his sports in high school—but out of a genuine love of the sport he had developed as a son of an NHL franchise president. He found the perfect fit in Boston University, the private school perched hard against the Charles River in the city's Fenway-Kenmore neighborhood.

Academically, it boasted a long line of Nobel and Pulitzer Prize winners and ranked annually among the top fifty schools in the nation. Athletically, it laid claim to one of the most storied hockey programs in the country, its skating Terriers having won multiple Division I championships since the team's founding in 1918.

As it happened, the Blackhawks were playing in Boston during Rocky's search, so Bill and Tommy Ivan joined Rocky for a tour of the area around the school. After the trio debriefed over dinner, it was decided. Rocky would spend two years at BU, then come home.

As he'd hoped, the change of scenery opened up a world of new experiences and different people—smart, driven, worldly people. He found them less immediately friendly than he was used to in the Midwest, more proper, but he admired their energy and ambition and, as usual, the people he met were charmed back. Because freshmen weren't allowed to have a car, he explored Boston in a way he never had in Chicago, via buses and the "T"—the famed subway system that deposited him at markets and historical sites such as Faneuil Hall and King's Chapel. Able to have wheels in his sophomore year, he ditched the old wood-paneled jalopy for something with a little more swagger, a rare indulgence for the otherwise frugal young Chicagoan. "I had a Chevy Chevette with a 395 engine," he recalls with a wistful inflection. "Yellow with black racing stripes. I thought I was pretty cool."

As in high school, however, his blazer and helmet-hair clashed sharply with the style more typical of the era, bell-bottom jeans, feathered locks, and army surplus jackets. But like that earlier era, too, his two roommates didn't seem to mind. It was a good thing because the threesome shared tight quarters in one of the school's high-rise dorms, providing yet another first for Rocky: learning to live with roommates.

Bob Jordan, Rocky's childhood friend who dropped by for a visit, recalls the group as a kind of Odd Couple with an extra Oscar Madison. Apparently, Rocky's clean-cut appearance initially brought puzzled reactions from his less starchy roommates, but his easygoing personality carried the day. "There these guys were with hair down to their waist, wearing tie-dye and playing the guitar and listening to the Grateful Dead, probably smoking some of that wacky tobacky," Jordan says. "And there's Rocky, with his stay-pressed hair and stay-pressed clothes, sitting there cracking jokes."

One moment, in particular, captured the peculiar dynamic. "I remember there was this party and they're all doing what they did," Jordan recalls, "and Rocky brings out a carpet sweeper and starts sweeping up. It was pure Rocky. He always had to have some sense of order." And yet he could fit in with ease with those who didn't.

Rocky's appearance, however, owed to more than innate preference. Walter Goldstein thinks that even then Rocky understood that he was representing more than himself, that he bore the weight of the Wirtz name and the burden of the heir apparent. That's not to say he was earnest to a fault—that he didn't like fun and even light excursions into mischief. Indeed, it was his ability to relate to just about anyone—and put them at their ease—that won him acceptance into most any group. At the same time, "we all kind of knew Rocky was being groomed for his position in the family business and, of course, he did too," Goldstein says.

Rocky may have found a way to fit in, but the East Coast reserve he encountered—and a summer job back in Chicago—confirmed where his heart lay. He was no Yankee. He was a Midwesterner, a Chicagoan, and always would be. The job involved working on the docks of the family wholesale liquor distributorship, Judge & Dolph. During those relatively carefree months, he traversed the city and suburbs, seeing places and things and people he had never really given much thought to before. Alleys for one, 1,900 miles of them, those narrow lanes behind row houses and apartment buildings where kids played stick ball and cars squeezed past each other and dads sizzled steaks on portable grills and, less appetizingly, rats skittered. The kitchens of fancy restaurants for another. Rocky had assumed they were all the same—spotless, bustling, delicacies boiling in shining pots. Some were, some weren't. Some were pigsties that any self-respecting inspector would have closed immediately, unless his palms were greased by the kind of green you didn't put in salads. South Side, North Side, West Side. The flat accents (FLAYet EEakksens) much more pleasant on his ear than the somewhat snootier park-the-car (Pahk the kah) patois of Hah-vuhd Yahd.

He liked the guys and the physical labor—grunting a hand truck of boxes up a ramp, no one special, just one of the fellas, accepted on his merits, rather than the boss's son sent to slum it for a while so he could brag that he got his hands dirty. In fact, "no one knew who I was," he recalls. "I think they suspected I was related to someone in management, they just didn't know who." About halfway through the summer his cover was blown when a crew member caught a glimpse of Bill in the paper and noted his strong resemblance. "Eventually they put two and two together," Rocky shrugs, but by then he was just another good guy with a strong back. "Nothing changed," he says. "Some of the drivers would milk overtime. I wouldn't say anything. That was between them and their supervisor. And, hey," he said with a sidelong look, "I'd get my fair share of that too."

True to his plan, he left BU after two years and enrolled at the school he'd always longed to attend. As a communications major at Northwestern, he fit right in again, adding frat boys to the hippies, New York hot shots, dockworkers, and pro athletes he'd encountered along the way to a growing list of friends. "I was living in a dormitory in a single room," he recalls. It was his first taste of true independence, so it was on him now to find ways to meet new folks. For recreation, he joined the recently formed Northwestern University Rugby Club. For companionship, he pledged the Phi Delta Theta fraternity—the Phi Delts.

Though he chose to stay in his dorm rather than move into the fraternity house, he proved an indispensible brother, for one important reason if nothing else. "I was the oldest one there, and at twenty-one could drink legally my junior year," he says, "which means I could buy liquor for all the guys."

Rocky earned his degree in 1975, but, unlike Bill, had no hesitation about entering the family business, though not the hockey end. For a variety of reasons—not the least of which joining the team's front office would put him directly in his father's line of fire—the liquor operation offered a better fit. Working on the docks and coming to know the rank and file—and taking field trips with Bill when he was younger—fed his love of building relationships. He also relished the thought of traveling to the various outposts of the business—Las Vegas, New York, California—and broadening his experience through those trips.

One other development argued for launching his Wirtz Corp. career: during his junior year at Northwestern, Rocky had gone on a double date with an attractive young blonde woman named Kathleen Whiston. The two had much in common. Both their fathers and grandfathers were involved in real estate. Kathy's father, Jerome Whiston, developed and managed prominent Loop skyscrapers. Her grandfather, Frank, was both a real estate mogul and president of the Chicago Board of Education under Mayor Richard J. Daley. Rocky and Kathy hit it off and were married on May 24, 1975, at

Faith, Hope, and Charity Catholic Parish in Winnetka, with a reception after at the private Sunset Ridge Country Club.

Though their union would yield three children—Danny, Hillary, and Kendall—the couple, despite their similar backgrounds, would prove an ill-conceived match. Marriage devolved into a separation, separation into a bitter divorce. Adding to the pain, the breakup would play out on the front page of the *Chicago Sun-Times* in a lengthy story that paraded battles petty and intimately personal before the public, a mortifying moment for all involved.

Meanwhile, Rocky found himself involved in a different type of family embarrassment—this one involving his younger brother, Peter. Tall, thin, athletic, and handsome, Peter hovered on the edge of the circle of Rocky and his friends. Though the two rarely quarreled, they never developed a close bond, the seven-year age difference—as well as diametrically opposed personalities—proving too wide a gulf.

Whereas Rocky embraced his high school years, Peter, to the dismay of their parents, dropped out at sixteen. To the greater consternation of their parents, he moved in with a substantially older woman, in her early thirties, according to family and friends close to the family. The relationship roiled the entire family. The parents were furious, both over the age difference between Peter and the woman—seriously inappropriate in their view—and Peter's decision to abandon school and home. "It was terrible," Rocky recalls. "Our parents told him either you break off the relationship with her and go to prep school or move out." Peter left.

Rocky shared his parents' fury. To him, Peter's affair was reckless, self-destructive, and toxic, not to mention deeply hurtful toward Bill, Joan, and their sisters. Rocky also saw the fling as a slap to the family, to Bill, to Arthur, to everything the father and grandfather had built.

At a Christmas party thrown by Bill, Rocky, having stewed for months, showed up spoiling for a showdown. "I had it out for him," Rocky admits. "I took him in the other room and I said, 'What are you doing?' " Rocky shoved Peter, then grabbed his tie and pulled. "I got it up to his Adam's apple and punched him," Rocky recalls. "I said, 'Lesson one, don't ever wear a tie to a fist fight.' " Rocky then verbally laid into his brother, a withering barrage that left Rocky red faced and trembling.

Recounting the story decades later, Rocky acknowledges that, no matter what his brother had done, it wasn't his best moment. He needed to confront Peter, but regrets that his temper so got the best of him. Eventually, Peter did leave the woman and he apologized, to his parents. If anything, as Rocky sees it, Peter swung from that lone moment of rebellion to the other extreme: complete, unquestioning obedience, particularly towards Bill. He moved back home and ultimately joined the family business, working for an independent beer distributorship and later running his own concessions firm and, later still, joining his family's business and overseeing all off-ice functions for the Blackhawks as a senior vice president.

As for the scuffle, the brothers rarely spoke of it and on the surface reached a sort of détente that remained mostly genial. But the wound cut deeply, so deeply it never fully healed. "From there," says Rocky, "our relationship was never the same."

Bill Grabs the Puck

As a freshly minted groom and Northwestern University graduate, Rocky Wirtz was a young man in a hurry. The ink had barely dried on his diploma and marriage certificate when—at age twenty-two in the summer of 1975—he and Kathy packed their things to move to New York City.

The day after a Bermuda honeymoon the couple boarded a plane to the Big Apple in high spirits, eager to begin their new life. They never intended to live in New York permanently. Rocky planned to spend a year there soaking up as much of the liquor trade as he could—grateful for the chance to do so away from the inevitable pressures he would face as the son of the boss once he joined Wirtz Corp.—before returning home to Chicago to begin his career in earnest.

Apart from the glittering thrill of going to work each day amid the hurly-burly of Midtown, life as a New Yorker was something less than glamorous for a couple lacking a Central Park West budget. Rocky, as was the plan, started at the bottom, with an entry-level job gathering trade research for another family conglomerate with major liquor interests, Joseph E. Seagram & Sons.

The company's headquarters offered a measure of glitz—designed by Mies van der Rohe, 375 Park Avenue had been hailed as an architectural masterpiece when it opened in 1958. (As it happened, Rocky arrived two years after the opening of a strikingly similar building in Chicago: van der Rohe's IBM Building.) But for Rocky, trips to that beautiful edifice were rare. Clinging to the lower rungs of Seagram, he toiled instead out of more pedestrian digs at 800 Third Avenue, "where they put us peons."

Home in those days was a rent-controlled one-bedroom apartment sublet from a friend of the family, a "typical Manhattan bachelor pad," as Rocky recalls it. Indeed, the place languished in a charmless brown brick building on a cheerless stretch of East Fifty-Sixth Street. Its Midtown location helped. Within a block in any direction beckoned a potpourri of restaurants, shops, and nightclubs, though many lay outside the bounds of the couple's modest budget.

Its biggest advantage was its distance from Chicago and a mammoth controversy that was brewing with the hockey team Rocky's father now ran, an episode that would become one of the most ignominious episodes in the history of the Blackhawks.

Three years earlier, in 1972, a group of investors hoping to compete with the NHL had formed the rogue World Hockey Association. One of its top priorities was to lure big names from the established league and none was bigger—or more prime for poaching, it turned out—than "the most famous Blackhawk of them all," as one scribe called him: Bobby Hull.

Despite his undeniable value to the team and the NHL, Hull's $100,000 salary fell well below market value—and he let Bill Wirtz and anyone else who would listen know it. "I had been at war with the Blackhawks' management for years," Hull later recalled in an interview with *Sports Illustrated*. "We hated each other."

Hull's animosity arose partly from a humiliation visited upon him after months of battling with the team's front office. He'd held out through the start of the 1969 season, threatening to retire. Team officials remained unmoved and called his bluff.

Hull caved, but the Hawks weren't going to let him off easy. Before he could suit up again, management told him, he would have to apologize. In public. Thus occurred a humiliating press conference in which Hull was hauled before a group of reporters at the Bismarck Hotel to personally apologize to Bill, general manager Tommy Ivan, and coach Billy Reay. *Tribune* columnist David Condon described the Appomattox in a story headlined "Armageddon: Lights. Camera. Action! Hull Surrenders." As "Hull strode in his face showed the scars of hundreds of hockey games," Condon wrote. "His smile seemed borrowed from a wax museum. Bobby resembled a former heavyweight boxing champion posing for photographs the day after he lost the title."

The truce, however, didn't hold. Almost immediately both sides started sniping again, opening wider a window for the World Hockey Association to swoop in and steal the pride-wounded superstar. The Winnipeg Jets made the offer—a contract that would more than double Hull's salary to $250,000 and add a $1 million signing bonus, payable up front. The deal shocked even Hull. "I thought it was a joke," he recalled in an interview years later. "I pretended to go along with it, just to scare Chicago. Then my agent, Harvey Weinberg, said, 'Bobby, these guys are serious.'" So badly did the fledgling league want Hull, in fact, that its other owners pitched in to cover the bonus.

Still, many regarded the notion that Hull would leave the Blackhawks—or more to the point, that the Blackhawks would allow him to leave without a serious counterproposal—as preposterous. For months, the Hawks played coy. And when management did make an eleventh-hour proposal, it was too late. Hull rejected it, prompting the Hawks to visit a final indignity on him. They sued him to prevent him from playing for the Jets.

The suit was later dropped, but the damage had been done. On June 28, 1972, Hull made it official, signing a ten-year contract with the Jets for what at the time was a staggering $2.75 million, plus the $1 million bonus. More lastingly, he declared his old team all but dead to him, blasting the front office—Bill more than anyone—for years to come.

Curiously, given his almost Pavlovian tendency to punch back, Bill Wirtz offered no public comment. In the decades to come—to his grave and beyond, in fact—the moment would blossom into a permanent stain on his reputation and an ignominious mark on the Wirtz name itself. As it happens, history will record that the prime mover in the fiasco was not Bill, but Arthur. "Bill took most of the heat for it and also was the one who admitted at the end it was a great mistake—as did Bobby," says Verdi, the Blackhawks historian. "But Arthur was a hard-ass. The Wirtz theory, basically Arthur's theory, was that if you pay Bobby what he wants then everybody's going to want a raise."

Cemented into place by the media of the day, however, the narrative hardened: Bill was a stubborn, bullying tightwad who ripped the heart out of Chicago fans by letting a beloved athlete and the best player in the history of the game skate away to a moose-country locale most could not even place on a map.

As the debacle unfolded, Rocky could only be grateful he had not been around—or, God forbid, involved—and feel vindicated in his decision to stay away from the Blackhawks in any professional capacity so long as his father ran the team. Still, he was a Wirtz and nothing, not eight hundred miles of separation nor the rightful claim that he had nothing to do with the Hull farce, could change his intimate connection to that suddenly dirty word: Wirtz.

• • •

Indeed, when Rocky returned to Chicago in 1976, it was to a city whose hockey fans were still livid at his father. In a transparent attempt to make up for the loss of Hull, Bill signed free agent Bobby Orr, a genuine superstar who had enjoyed a stellar career with the Boston Bruins. Among his accolades were eight straight Norris trophies, awarded to the league's best defenseman, and three consecutive Hart trophies for most valuable player.

Orr was coming off major knee surgery, however—one of several in his career—and over the next three years he played only twenty-six games and missed the entire 1977–78 season, having undergone so many knee surgeries (more than a dozen) that he struggled to walk, much less skate. Orr tried to stage a comeback in 1979, but called it quits after just six games. He was done.

The result was that rather than repairing his reputation, or helping the fans forget the clumsy handling of *l'affair de Hull*, Bill only poured gasoline on the growing brushfire of anger blazing around him.

Rocky, watching it all unfold from afar, remained mercifully out of the fray. Having taken a job at Judge & Dolph, he worked out of the company's Clybourn headquarters on the city's North Side, a firewall from the fraught atmosphere at 1800 West Madison. More than geography spared him the Blackhawks taint. His boss—a director named Joe Flick—was a far less volatile presence than Bill and what's more, the liquor business, though far more lucrative, didn't operate under the public microscope trained on the Blackhawks' every move. Rocky was also able to climb the corporate ladder far more quickly there. In fact, two years after he joined Judge & Dolph, Flick retired, lifting Rocky to the position of vice president.

For the moment, he and Kathy still lived relatively modestly. From 1976 to 1980, home was a two-bedroom apartment in the southeast corner of Evanston. The building, owned by Wirtz Realty, "was a typical Evanston walk-up," Rocky recalls. "We had two cars, which we parked in a public lot next to us. There were parks and stuff nearby and we could walk to the lake."

The nearby amenities soon came in handy. Rocky's son, Danny, was born in 1977, which meant Kathy could take the newborn for strolls along the lake while Rocky jetted off to meetings at the various branches of the Wirtz liquor business in California, Minnesota, Wisconsin, and eventually Las Vegas and Reno.

When Kathy became pregnant with Hillary in 1979, however, the couple knew they needed to find a real home. They settled on a charming two-story white brick house on an acre lot in Winnetka, not far from Rocky's childhood home on De Windt, where Bill and Joan still lived. Arthur helped Rocky come up with the down payment, though not without needling him. "Why do you have a mortgage?" Arthur asked.

"Because I can't afford the whole thing," Rocky replied.

"Well, what happens if you lose your job?"

"Are you trying to tell me something?" Rocky, trying to lighten the moment, recalls saying.

"No," came the gruff reply. "I just believe in paying cash for everything."

The Baron of the Bottom Line never abandoned that belief. He also never cottoned to losses, rare as they were. In fact, Arthur's knack for picking winners was almost uncanny, with one exception (beyond the Hopalong Cassidy debacle)—a miscalculation that led Rocky to take one of the biggest risks in his early career.

Arthur had bought a warehouse in an industrial area in San Francisco. He planned to store liquor there from Rathjen Bros., a wholesaler owned by the family in the Bay Area. Rathjen—among the businesses that Rocky oversaw—was not doing well. "California was a tough place," Rocky explains. "Your receivables, your inventory was high. Just the general market. It was hard to make money." Because of that, much of the massive warehouse sat empty. "We had the whole back end vacant," Rocky recalls. "About fifty thousand to sixty thousand square feet."

He didn't want to tell Arthur that Rathjen was struggling and face the inevitable wrath, so he came up with a slightly sneaky solution. "I sublet the warehouse to a wicker furniture manufacturer to help cover losses."

One day, perhaps sensing something was amiss, Arthur told Rocky that he wanted to take his wife to San Francisco for the weekend and visit the warehouse to see what it looked like. Rocky blanched. "If you sublet someone's real estate—even if it's your grandfather's real estate—and don't tell them about it, and, not only don't tell them about it, don't even give them the proceeds, that's grounds for dismissal. As in, you're fired."

Rocky managed to stammer out, "That's wonderful. Anything I can do for you?"

No, Arthur said. "I'll see you in two days."

Rocky immediately launched a covert operation worthy of *The Sting*. "I called the wicker company and told them, 'We've got to get any trace of furniture out of here. Take the signs down. Put everything on semis. Whatever it costs. Broom sweep that thing clean, and don't let anyone know.'" And by the way, he added, "You've got two days to do it."

The scheme worked. "We got everything out of there. When Arthur came back to Chicago, he never talked about it," says Rocky. "It was so over the line, but I was desperate. I knew if I'd gone to my grandfather to sublease the space, he would have taken the money and that would have defeated the purpose. I never shared it with my dad. Whether Arthur knew what I'd done, I don't know."

By late 1982, the episode was forgotten, replaced by more immediate concerns: Arthur's health was failing. The issues plaguing him included diabetes and a variety of other ailments, including heart problems. Earlier in the year, he'd been hospitalized for weeks after contracting a staph infection during surgery to install a pacemaker.

By the time doctors cleared the infection, Arthur had been bedridden for so long that one of his legs had atrophied. "They told him he'd never walk again," Rocky says. But in a last show of the old fire, the old lion rallied. "He said, 'I'm not going to be a cripple just because you told me I am.'" Rocky says that his grandfather checked himself into the Rehabilitation Institute of Chicago and relearned to walk.

There was no recovering from an event that occurred just after Christmas of 1982, however. Virginia Wadsworth Wirtz, Arthur's wife of fifty-six years, unexpectedly died in her sleep at seventy-nine. An article in the *Tribune* the next day noted Virginia's tireless work with charities, from the American Cancer Society to the Illinois Children's Home to the American Heart Fund. Calling her the Blackhawks' "number one fan," the article cited the time in 1967 when she "braved the worst snow storm in Chicago history to watch her beloved team beat Toronto." After her funeral, held at Fourth Presbyterian, Arthur collapsed at the farm from a severe stroke and was placed on a ventilator.

Bad begat worse. In early 1983, Rocky's mother, Joan, was diagnosed with an aggressively metastasizing cancer. She died only a few months later, in May, at Michael Reese Hospital and Medical Center. "She was a lady who was elite but never acted as if she were better than anyone," one woman who'd worked with her to raise money for a Des Plaines children's home told the *Tribune*.

Two months after that, on July 21, Arthur Wirtz died at eighty-two in Henrotin Hospital on Oak Street downtown. He had been hospitalized since his collapse at the burial services for Virginia. "He literally could not recover from her death," says Rocky.

The passing of three members of the family in a short span left no member of the surviving Wirtz family untouched. The implications of each death, wrenching as they were, ranged far beyond mere grief and loss.

To wit: under terms of the succession plan, Bill was now head of Wirtz Corp., with his younger brother, Michael, next in line. On a much more personal level, Joan's death marked a change in Bill that would manifest for the rest of his life. "Mom had helped Dad stay grounded," Rocky says. "After her death, he wasn't the same and would never be the same." Stated another way—without the one check on his temper, a calming presence with whom Bill could share the burdens and pressures of his high intensity professional world, he began a long descent into a darker and darker place.

The Penalty Box

To the world at large, the death of Arthur Wirtz marked the passing of a titan. Almost by sheer force of will, he had reached into the depths of the Great Depression and fashioned from its rubble a shining city—his skyline of real estate, liquor, and entertainment a daily testimony to his legacy.

His years as owner of the Blackhawks and his vital role in growing the league had landed him in the Hockey Hall of Fame in 1971, soon to be followed by his son, Bill. His partnership with Sonja Henie had earned him recognition as "the father of arena entertainment." He was never officially King Arthur, of course, but he was recognized by royalty, having been awarded the Royal Order of St. Olav by King Olav V of Norway. And he did it all with the authority and swagger of a fading breed: the industrial tycoon.

To his family, Arthur's death signaled something more personally seismic: the ascendancy of the new paterfamilias, Bill.

Arthur had ruled with imperial edicts and a fierce temper, but he had largely done so without resorting to the kind of over-the-top public tantrums already displayed by his volatile son. As fearsome as Arthur could be, he would never have exiled his own flesh, much less maneuver to block the rightful heir to the throne. The new boss, Bill, had no such reluctance, according to the accounts of Rocky, a family member, and several people close to the family. In addition to hockey, Rocky and others say, Bill pushed the Blackhawks into a new business: "The grudge business."

Trying to characterize for how long, or how deeply Bill grieved for his father would be unfair. People process such moments differently—some with tears and long depressions and others bear up stoically while anguishing inside. And there is no suggestion that Bill was anything other than a loving and dutiful son to Arthur.

That said, his lone expression of public grief, captured by a reporter who was there, struck some as somewhat unsettling. The *Tribune* reported that Bill received word of the death at the Drake Hotel, as he was about to enter a meeting with the NHL Board of Governors. "William Wirtz took the message calmly," reporter Mike Conklin wrote. "He put the telephone down, tears beginning to well in his eyes, and retreated into a restroom. A few minutes later, he emerged composed, huddled with a few friends to relate the news, and charged into the meeting to conduct a five-hour session in businesslike manner."

The most telling hint that Arthur's death had an effect on Bill's psyche revealed itself when the son returned to work at the 680 North Lake Shore Drive headquarters of Wirtz Corp. Despite his new title of chairman, Bill refused to move into the office of the former chairman—his father—or change anything about it or the boardroom where King Arthur's round table stood in silent rebuke of anyone who dared question the Founder. Bill similarly left Arthur's rules untouched, most famously Arthur's refusal to air regular-season home games on TV. In doing so, Bill adopted his father's reasoning down the line: that showing the games was akin to giving away the product, was unfair to the faithful who did buy tickets, and discouraged fans from coming to the stadium. The logic may have made reasonable sense in Arthur's time. But by the 1970s and 1980s, it had been proved demonstrably wrong, as indicated by the fact that virtually every team in every sport aired their home games.

And far from keeping fans away, TV exposure actually encouraged them to come to the stadium. What Arthur—and Bill—failed to see, or acknowledge, was that the televised broadcasts were a two- or three-hour commercial for the brand, a platform from which owners could create a narrative about how they wanted their franchise to be perceived—as high-flying, as blue collar, as tough . . . as winners. During those broadcasts, teams could sell their merchandise, announce special events and giveaways, and steer fans' attention to other attractions at the stadium.

Such benefits created a sort of multiplier effect: able to watch the games, fans followed their teams more closely, and in turn came to care more about the players and their individual stories as well as found themselves wanting to join the excitement at the stadium. Part of that excitement was wearing the team's gear—especially true of the Blackhawks with their beloved Indian head logo—which meant more merchandise sales.

Less tangible, but just as potent, underlies an even more compelling argument. The analogy may not be perfect, but consider a concert featuring a favorite musical artist—the Beatles, say. You could listen to them any time by just dropping a record on the phonograph or by turning on the radio. You could see them on a variety show such as *Ed Sullivan*. But are any of these things remotely the same as a live performance? Taking the analogy a step further, would hearing the Beatles on a record or the radio, or seeing them on the *Ed Sullivan Show*, make a concert sellout any less likely?

The Blackhawks were not the Beatles (though many years later they would often be compared to rock stars), but the argument applied. Defending the anti-TV line ignores the X factor of shared experience—that is, the thrill of sitting among thousands of like-minded fans, beer in hand, cheering your team (or booing them, as may be the case); elbowing the guy next to you after a good play; clapping the back of a fellow zealot after a goal; the pride of being able to say, "Oh, the game? I was there."

At the very least, in the case of the Blackhawks, if Bill had reversed Arthur and put the games on television, the gesture would likely have generated such mammoth goodwill that everything—the animosity of the Bobby Hull and Bobby Orr debacles, the unhinged rants, the less-than-stellar seasons—may have faded if not disappeared. With a word—OK—Bill could have gone from hated to heroic.

Instead, the new owner, if anything, dug in his heels deeper. What truly rankled wasn't just his obstinacy but the defiance in that stubbornness, the sense of delight he seemed to take in tweaking the fans. That arrogance, as much as anything, hastened his devolution from simply being unpopular—a status not exactly foreign to sports franchise owners—to something darker: being a villain. The media picked up the cudgel with glee and pounded Bill with it mercilessly. Thus are caricatures born. And no one was lampooned more often, more cruelly, more unsparingly than Bill Wirtz (a rogue publication called the *Blue Line*, sold outside the stadium on game days, made a living off disparaging Bill in the most vicious, nasty, personal ways possible).

Lest he be painted as a victim, let it be clearly said that much if not most of the criticism against Bill was deserved. And let it also be said that he often brought it on himself. For some reason, when presented with two choices, one that might resonate with fans or one almost guaranteed to irritate them, he invariably chose the latter. "Club presidents aren't in the business of being loved by fans," was Bill's go-to response. "I learned that from my father."

Bill had a point there, too. Making decisions to please the whims of columnists—or worse, overheated fans—was madness. So, too, however, was ignoring a unanimous clamor for something like airing the games on TV.

The family, particularly Peter, watched the way their father was treated in the press with growing vexation. At luncheons, at City Hall, when Bill was making yet another donation of a million dollars or more to one of the many beneficiaries of Wirtz Corp. largesse, he was treated with honor and dignity.

Open the paper, and he was a bum.

What mattered at the moment, practically speaking at least, were the further implications of Arthur's death. Bill was, without question, head of the company. Next in succession after Bill was Bill's less-well-known brother Michael. Five years Bill's junior, with softer features that included a round face, a wide, open smile, dark hair, and an ample frame reminiscent of grandfather Arthur, the unofficial dossier on Michael was that he was the "nicer" Wirtz brother. And indeed, he was far quieter, almost never given to angry outbursts, and seemed for less ambitious than Bill. Still, as with Bill, as with any human being, really, a superficial list of descriptors falls woefully short in fully capturing the man.

A graduate of the University of Pennsylvania's Wharton School of Business, renowned as among the best business schools in the country, Michael had spent years as vice president of the Blackhawks, vice president of Wirtz Corp. and of Wirtz Realty, and as an alternate governor of the NHL. Operating almost exclusively behind the scenes, he nonetheless wielded considerable influence over the one person few would have guessed. "He was my right-hand man," Bill told *Crain's Chicago Business* in a 1997 interview. "On account of the succession agreement, I had the voting stock, but we were like partners."

"He was sort of the Bill whisperer," Bruce Wirtz MacArthur recalls. "If I was ever going to try to persuade Bill of anything, I would go to Michael Wirtz. We were fortunate to have him because you could go to Michael and say, 'Can you go talk to your brother a little bit, because he's a little out of control.' And he would. In his own way, he could say, 'You know, Bill . . .' And Bill would listen."

Though Rocky was never close to Michael, he deeply admired his quiet strength and openness to reason and found himself wondering more than once how the team might fare differently under such a steadying influence.

As it was, Rocky was profoundly grateful for an action Michael took on Rocky's behalf early in his career: "He made sure that Dad made me an officer of each of the family's companies. Not only the liquor companies, but all the companies—including the Blackhawks," Rocky says. That single, simple, under-the-radar move, Rocky says, may have done as much to establish him as a force to be reckoned with in Wirtz Corp. as Arthur's plan of succession.

Rocky's relationship with his father was far closer, of course, but, as with anyone in Bill's orbit, complicated. Through much of his childhood, Rocky had enjoyed a closeness with Bill on which he still looks back fondly—those nights in the living room when Bill and Joan would hold court with his friends, the late nights at the Pump Room hanging out with Bill and Jimmy Norris, Bill traveling with Rocky to pick out a college, the father's insistence that Rocky tag along on business trips. Whereas Peter threw his parents into chaos with his ill-advised relationship, Rocky hewed to a largely prescribed plan that would have made Arthur proud—and Bill was grateful.

Still, almost from the start, friction marked the interactions between father and son, bad blood that went beyond the normal strain between a stern father and a headstrong son. Whereas most men capitulated to Bill without question—rightly fearful of the consequences—Rocky insisted on speaking his mind, speaking honestly but bluntly.

But standing up to Bill at home was one thing. When Rocky confronted Bill in a professional context, as he would come to find out, the ramifications were severe unto draconian.

• • •

In 1987, four years after Joan's death, Bill married Alice Pirie Hargrave—"Ittie," to most everyone, a member of the Carson Pirie Scott department store family and the ex-wife of the son of a founder of Merrill Lynch. Bill had long been a drinker, but in 1991 his tippling led to an arrest for driving under the influence. Bill pleaded guilty and in 1992 was sentenced to a year's court supervision, fined $500, and had his license suspended for three months. "You're fortunate there was an officer there to stop you before you killed yourself or someone else," Cook County Circuit Court Judge Jerome Orbach lectured Bill in the Skokie Courthouse, one of the few times in Bill's life that someone other than Arthur dared scold him with such blunt force.

How much of a role the trio of deaths—Joan's, Virginia's, and Arthur's—contributed to his drinking is impossible to know. One unusual consequence of Arthur's passing, however, was clear: it dramatically deepened Bill's relationship with his younger son. Since returning to the fold after the crisis of his romance with the older woman, Peter Wirtz had gained a sort of prodigal son's favor with Bill, largely, it seems, through Peter's efforts. At odds with his parents only a few years earlier, Peter took some courses at Lake Forest College (though he didn't graduate), then he briefly went to work as a brand manager for a beer company in Chicago.

At the age of twenty-three, the year of Arthur's death, Peter took over management of the concession contracts for Detroit's Tiger Stadium and three area racetracks. With Bill's help, Peter secured a seven-figure loan from a Detroit bank and founded Bismarck

Enterprises. The company initially flourished, particularly after Peter sold the Detroit contract in 1990 and moved into the Chicago market, taking over contracts for the old Chicago Stadium and other venues.

A 1996 *Tribune* profile drew a stark contrast between Peter and his father. "Unlike the rough-and-tumble, in-your-face personality associated with sports, hockey and the Wirtz family," Barbara Sullivan wrote, "Peter Wirtz is a tall, soft-spoken, deliberate man who politely calls his employees 'team members,' and doesn't drink, smoke, eat red meat, or ever clutter his desk."

His milder disposition, to say nothing of his utter devotion and absolute refusal to confront his father on any matter, personal or professional, deepened the growing bond between him and Bill. That same year, Bill named Peter to head a new marketing division for the Blackhawks, a first for an organization whose unofficial motto under Arthur had been "fannies first and marketing never." But beyond opening Hawk Quarters, a shop that sold the team's merchandise, nothing much in the way of bold new ideas surfaced.

All of it was fine by Rocky. Though he rooted for the Blackhawks and attended NHL Board of Governors meetings, his energies were consumed with expanding the wholesale wine and spirits operation. At the same time, his own family continued to grow. In 1986, he and Kathy had their third child, Kendall, and in 1990, they moved into a stately Georgian mansion in Winnetka.

But as Bill grew closer to Peter, Rocky's relationship with his father deteriorated. "He would lash out," Rocky says. There were the shouting matches, noisy arguments that in one case nearly led to physical blows between father and son. Most of the time the blowups were the result of Rocky pushing back on a Bill edict. Sometimes, Rocky caused the flare-up by merely expressing a contrary opinion.

More and more, Bill's tactic was to put his elder son in the "penalty box," as Rocky puts it. "He just wouldn't talk to you. And I mean it wouldn't be a couple months, it would be a year, two years. For months on end, he wouldn't pick up the phone, he wouldn't discuss stuff." As a result, Rocky attended fewer and fewer Blackhawks meetings. On the rare occasion he did show up, Bill either ignored his son's contributions or simply pretended he wasn't there. Eventually, Rocky stopped coming altogether.

The punishment overtook Rocky's family. "He would say, 'Don't bother to show up for Thanksgiving,'" Rocky recalls. The same for Christmas. "He'd say, 'Don't worry, I'll drop your Christmas presents off.' I told him, 'I don't need your Christmas presents.'"

Rocky's son, Danny, looks back at his grandfather Bill with mostly fond memories, but recalls receiving letters that were "very hurtful." Bill was "an extremely playful, adventurous, mischievous grandpa, especially when I was a young child," Danny says. "But there were also some things that really hurt me as I got older and our relationship got complicated."

The tensions with Rocky—indeed with the world—deepened after Bill suffered a serious stroke in February 1995—likely the result of his years as a chain-smoker and hard drinker. As it happened, the most frequent object of Bill's wrath, Rocky, was the person who saved his life. "I got a call from the housekeeper that Dad wasn't right so I came right over," Rocky recalls. "He wasn't able to pull his socks up and his right side was sagging and I said, 'Dad, I think you're having a stroke.'" Bill snarled at Rocky that he was fine, but Rocky summoned an ambulance.

Rocky then called his friend, Dr. Jeffrey Vender, an anesthesiologist with the Northshore University HealthSystem. Vender recalls, "He said, 'Jeff, I'm at dad's house. We think he had a stroke, they're going to bring him to Evanston.'" Tests revealed a clot the size of a fingertip hanging by a thread in the carotid artery in Bill's neck. The surgery to remove it would be risky. If even a piece broke off, the consequences would be fatal. On the other hand, Bill would almost certainly die if nothing was done. Rocky made the call: do the surgery. As it happened, Rocky also knew the surgeon on call, Dr. John Golan—the two having been friends since eighth grade. Bill groused that one of "Rocky's friends" would be his surgeon, even though Golan was renowned for his expertise on vascular procedures.

"It's a sad day when your friends are taking care of me," Vender recalls Bill saying to Rocky as he was being wheeled in to the operating room. "I'll never forget it."

The surgery, a procedure called a carotid endarterectomy, was a success and Bill slowly recovered. Six months later, when Bill had an unrelated seizure in the 680 offices, Rocky again called an ambulance that may have saved his father's life.

Rather than being grateful or relieved, Bill grew even more erratic and angry. "Certain right-side strokes can change your personality. And it certainly did with his," says Rocky. Another factor almost certainly contributed. Even after Bill's stroke, he continued to imbibe. After the seizure, however, realizing alcohol was getting the better of him, Bill quit cold turkey. The absence of alcohol, however, in no way softened his temper. In fact, if anything Bill acted out in even more troubling ways.

One such blowup came when he stormed into *Crain's Chicago Business* and unleashed a withering rant about a story that particularly incensed him. The article, mild compared to the blistering tone regularly used by the city's columnists, questioned Bill's push for a lockout against players in 2004 to check rising salaries. The article argued that the move "could further cripple a team that's fallen far from its glory days as one of the NHL's founding franchises." Bill, hands shaking with rage, roared at the assembled editors and writers.

In later years, Bill vented his anger through letters and faxes. "Grandpa was a prolific letter writer, but Dad would almost never write until his stroke," says Rocky. "After that, he was writing letters all the time. That was one of the biggest changes in his personality."

The pool of Bill's targets was vast and deep—from politicians to business leaders to family members to the commissioner of the NHL, Gary Bettman. Sitting in his spacious, sun-drenched corner office in midtown Manhattan, Bettman laughs at the recollection. In his case, Bill's choice of weapons was the fax machine. "I'd hear something arriving—you know that sound a fax makes—and I'd see the cover sheet with the Blackhawk logo scrolling up and the hair would stand up on the back of my neck," Bettman says. "Because I knew something was coming and it wasn't gonna be good."

Far and away, Bill's most impassioned and prolific targets were members of the media. Many times he would write a reporter or columnist directly. But he also routinely peppered the top executives at both major Chicago papers, the *Sun-Times* and the *Tribune*, with screeds against what he perceived as "below the belt" coverage, often urging them to upbraid or even reassign their writers.

No matter who the target, the missives invariably displayed a sharp wit, a sardonic tone, and a language and style that in some cases rose to the level of literary. Indeed, his attacks sometimes included references plucked from the classics: "To be sure, the Bears are the Brobdingnagians and we are the Lilliputians," he wrote to one editor, using the fictional terms employed by Jonathan Swift in *Gulliver's Travels* for giants versus tiny people.

An ugly incident during the 1999 season led to a sarcastic exchange with *Tribune* sports columnist Steve Rosenbloom, an admitted "smartass," according to his Twitter profile. Angry over what he believed was rough play by the Hawks, the general manager of the Washington Capitals, George McPhee, sucker punched Blackhawks coach Lorne Molleken outside the Hawks locker room.

After the attack (for which McPhee was suspended for a month without pay and fined $20,000), the Capitals coach, Ron Wilson, chimed in that had he known, he and his players would have been right behind McPhee. In response, addressed to Rosenbloom from "Moron," Bill challenged the Capitals to meet him in Chicago, "go into a room and turn out the lights and settle this."

In his column, Rosenbloom called Wirtz's challenge "inflammatory, thuggish and stupid." He said the Hawks owner "is displaying just that type of moronic leadership that explains why this organ-I-zation has gone without a Stanley Cup longer than any active team."

Wirtz fired off a memo to the columnist, saying in part: "Obviously, we share different values. Yours are always good, and mine are always evil. Howsoever, mine were good enough to be elected an honoured member of the Hockey Hall of Fame. After receiving this letter, I suppose you will lampoon this shrine." He signed the note, "From your moronic reader 'Sucker' Wirtz." He added, "P. S. I think I prefer being called 'Dollar Bill'—a name given to me by a class writer."

Following his father's lead, Peter wrote to Howard Tyner, then editor-in-chief of the *Tribune*, saying, "the constant barrage of 'below the belt shots' that Steve Rosenbloom has taken at us is at times, unbearable. I do not understand the humor and satire he uses. . . ." Peter enclosed a sampling of past articles by Rosenbloom and urged Tyner to review them. "Why does he need to constantly criticize our organization in this demeaning manner?" Bill Wirtz "does not deserve to be called a 'moron,'" Peter said.

If Bill thought the faxes and letters weren't sufficient, he would call. "I literally would be on the phone with him five, six hours a week," says Gary Bettman. "He would typically call late in the day, which is fine with me, five, six o'clock. My wife would call and ask my assistant, 'What time you think Gary is gonna be home?' And the standard line would be, 'He just got on with Mr. Wirtz,' which meant, eat dinner without me. Which was fine. I had no problem doing that.

"But if you disagreed with something with him, he would get angry, particularly in the later days. Even if you were right, it was hard to have a discussion."

When all else failed, Bill's outbursts became physical. "I remember at some point I had appointed him to the audit committee," Bettman says. "The first meeting, something came up—I can't remember the issue—but he got mad and he packed up his bag in the middle of the meeting and jumped up and went to make his exit from the room. Well, the door had a stationary handle. He grabbed with these massive hands of his and pulled and pulled and he ripped the thing out of the door. He's standing there holding the handle and he looked around and just put it on the floor and left. Nobody said a word."

John Miller, CEO of North American Corp. and a longtime Rocky friend, recalls an even more alarming episode during a meeting when Bill stood up in a rage, threw a chair, then marched over to the person running the gathering and said, "Let's finish this right here."

For Rocky, Bill's anger made an excruciating development in his life even worse. In 1997, Rocky separated from Kathy en route to a bitter divorce that was recounted in detail six years later in a lengthy article in the *Sun-Times*. The story laid bare a trove of embarrassing personal and financial information and detailed ugly and often petty squabbling over assets.

The divorce deepened Bill's anger toward his oldest son, Rocky says—not because of appearances or the publicity or any allegations made by or against Kathy, but because of the annoyance it caused Bill. "Her lawyers would do stuff just to aggravate him and it worked," Rocky says. During a deposition, for example, Kathy's attorneys asked Bill to divulge the terms of his will. He refused. "Then he'd get mad and take it out on me," Rocky says. "So for that seven-year period that it took to get divorced, he was really estranged from me. I was paying these astronomical legal bills personally and it wasn't pleasant. He never offered to help."

Bill also was infuriated that details of the Wirtz family finances, closely guarded from the start, had been splashed all over the front page of the *Sun-Times*. In response, Bill wrote a one-word letter to editor in chief Michael Cooke: "Thanks." Bill later explained in a follow-up missive to Cooke, the note "was not meant to be sarcastic, but rather to say I needed the printing [of the financial information] like a [*sic*] needed a hole in the head."

Amid the swirling tumult came news that for the moment, at least, united the family. In the fall of 1996, just at the start of the new Blackhawks season, Michael Wirtz was admitted to the University of Chicago Hospitals for treatment of an aggressive cancer that would claim his life within a few weeks. Mourners lamented the loss of "a very quiet man, a wonderful man." Florence Sewell, a friend, told the *Sun-Times*, "He was just a dear person, but very private, almost timid."

For Bill, Rocky, and Peter, the death made for yet more anguish during an already difficult time. It also carried with it a seismic implication that escaped no one, least of all Rocky and Bill: Rocky now stood first in line to inherit the company his father fervently wanted to deny him.

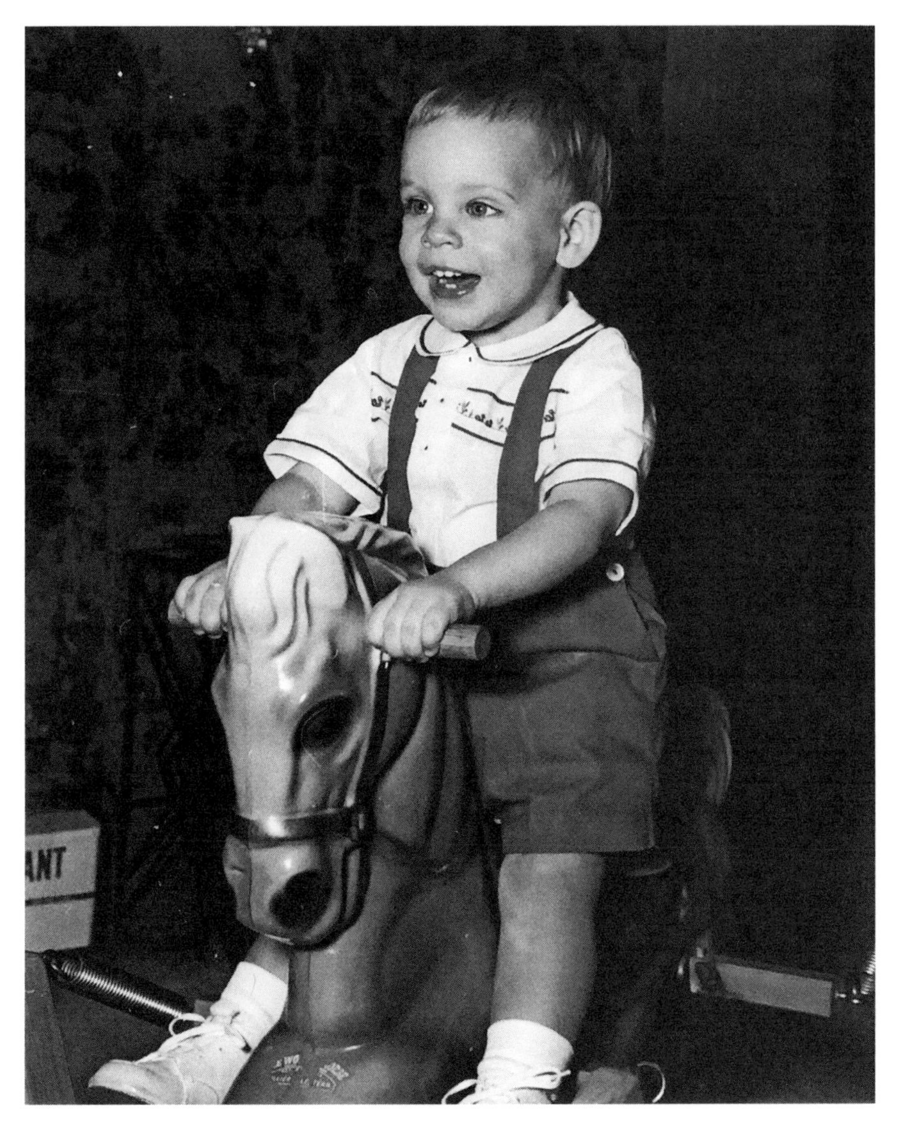

Rocky, approximately two years old

Rocky, age six, seated to the right of sisters Gail and Karey

The family in their Winnetka home (*clockwise from the top of the stairs*): Rocky, Gail, Peter, Bill, Joan, Alison, and Karey

Seventeen-year-old Rocky and actor Hugh O'Brian (a close friend of Joan "Jo" and Bill Wirtz) stand on either side of Blackhawks legend Bobby Hull, who holds an award presented to him by O'Brian.

Engagement portrait of Arthur's wife, Virginia (*née* Wadsworth) in 1924. Arthur and Virginia were married for fifty-seven years.

Arthur prepares to board a Trans World Airlines flight, on his way to the pioneer of all ice shows, his annual Hollywood Ice Revue. What began in 1935 as a $14,000 production that played for two nights in the Chicago Stadium quickly became a sensation, with a production budget of $1 million—more than four times that of a Broadway show at the time—that attracted more than three million fans each year.

Arthur with the skater extraordinaire and international celebrity Sonja Henie. In 1940, the pair convinced G. S. Eyssell, the director of Radio City Music Hall, to convert the Center Theatre to an ice theater, in what was considered the most daring experiment in New York theatrical history. The Center Theatre's ice productions were wildly successful.

Arthur, seated next to partner Jimmy Norris, at Madison Square Garden

Arthur, chomping a hamburger, in the stands at the Chicago Stadium with partner Jimmy Norris

Arthur in Miami on the sixty-five-foot *Blackhawk*, the forerunner to a 123-foot version of the yacht that is used by the family today

Arthur reading the program for his rodeo show featuring film star Hopalong Cassidy

Arthur (*right*) with partner Jimmy Norris. In between them, superstar player Bobby Hull clowns around in his original number 16 jersey from his first few years with the Blackhawks (1957 to 1961). Hull later switched to number 7 and again to the now-retired number 9 as a tribute to his idol Gordie Howe.

Arthur, NHL president Clarence Campbell, and Jimmy Norris with the 1961 Stanley Cup after the Blackhawks' championship run. It would be forty-nine years before the Blackhawks won another cup.

Arthur flanked by his two sons, Arthur Michael Wirtz Jr. and William (Bill) Wirtz

Bill Wirtz, his wife, Joan, and his mother, Virginia, with Bobby Hull, celebrating a goal in the Chicago Stadium

Bill Wirtz on the ice with hall of fame goalie Tony Esposito in the early '70s for the annual team photo taken before the Blackhawks' practice

Bill Wirtz with Blackhawks legend and Hall of Famer Stan Mikita, celebrating his 500th career goal in 1977

Bill Wirtz holding his first grandchild—Rocky's son, Danny Wirtz—at his home in Winnetka in 1978

Rocky with his wife, Marilyn Wirtz (*née* Queen)

Rocky (*far right*) with father, Bill, and younger brother, Peter, at the United Center in 2000 after taking the annual team photo

Free Fall

The slow-motion death spiral of the Chicago Blackhawks from the heights of a premiere franchise to the depths of bungling and failure seemed to track precisely with the hastening decline of the club's progressively combative and erratic owner, Bill Wirtz.

In the years that followed his 1969 public meltdown, the Blackhawks, to Bill's credit, maintained a level of excellence by reaching the Stanley Cup finals three times, in 1971, 1973, and 1992. And though the team lost each time, its twenty-eight-year streak of making the playoffs—just one trip shy of the all-time NHL record of twenty-nine held by the Boston Bruins—marked an achievement for Bill that no amount of criticism can gainsay.

Still, entering the 1997–98 campaign, the media and hockey experts sensed that the upcoming season might be the one that ended the run. As it was, the Hawks had barely squeaked into the playoffs the year before, their 34–35–13 record earning just enough points to qualify as the Western Conference's final seed, and the team lost in the quarterfinals. Barely a month into the new season, the pessimism seemed to be justified. With a 2–0 loss to the St. Louis Blues on October 17, the Hawks fell to 0–7, matching one of the club's most ignominious records: most losses to open a season. Over that stretch, the team had more losses than goals scored (six).

The recriminations came fast and from all quarters, including the coach. "It's a familiar scene, it's a familiar feeling, and it's a sick feeling," said Craig Hartsburg, who would be sacked in a year, spinning a hiring and firing merry-go-round that would include four different coaches in as many seasons. "We make a mistake and it ends up in the net."

The *Tribune's* Rich Strom noted that "Chris Chelios fired the puck toward an empty St. Louis Blues net after picking up a cross-checking penalty . . . and missed. That sums up the Blackhawks' season from hell."

Indeed. At the end of the season, the Hawks finished next to last in their division and were shut out a league-high eleven times. The team ended the campaign almost identically to the way they began it—by going winless (with one tie) in their last seven games. And for the first time in almost three decades, the Hawks did indeed miss the playoffs.

The postmortems spared no one. "What's wrong with the Blackhawks goes a lot deeper than a team short on talent, character, heart, hitting and all the other ingredients necessary for a successful hockey club," the *Daily Herald*'s Tim Sassone, perhaps the city's most influential hockey reporter, wrote in a withering indictment. "The demise of the Hawks didn't just happen overnight. This club had been mismanaged and on a downward spiral" for two years.

That last observation was portentous, hinting, as it did, that the bottom had yet to be reached. And indeed, the franchise's slide into the lowest rung of sports purgatory—irrelevance—was only beginning. The "season from hell," as the *Sun-Times* put it, was about to become the decade from hell.

And so it was. One dreadful finish followed another. Hartsburg joined the ranks of the ignominiously sacked, followed by yet more successors, each announced with fanfare followed by a shove out the door:

—Dirk Graham, the longtime Blackhawks defenseman hired after one year as an assistant ("I played with the guy. I knew what kind of leadership he has," Bob Murray, Chicago's general manager, boasted. "I know the kind of instantaneous respect he commands when he walks in the locker room.") Gone after one season.

—Lorne Molleken, also a former player, remembered mostly for getting socked in the eye by Washington Capitals general manager George McPhee after a preseason game. Also fired after one season.
—Alpo Suhonen, ripped by the city's columnists for his lack of discipline, did not even last a whole season, having retired with "heart issues" before the inevitable guillotine drop.
—Bob Pulford, nearly as reviled by fans as Bill, given a seventh try on the bench, moved out after a third-place finish that left the team in the playoff cold yet again.

During that stretch, in a league where postseason berths were something akin to participation ribbons, the Blackhawks could not eke out a single appearance.

The shocking decline mirrored Bill's descent into his own kind of abyss. In his feistier days, when he could defend himself with the shield of the team's successes, he delighted in needling reporters, editors, and fans in press conferences and on the pages of the city's dailies. After his stroke, and as the franchise stumbled year after disheartening year, he retreated into a far more insular world populated only be the unquestioningly loyal—Peter, Pulford, and a small group of others. He showed up at the offices of 680 North Lake Shore later and later in the day and on game nights bunkered himself into the private room off the Sonja Henie lounge, inviting in only his most trusted inner circle. Rocky did not make the cut, though he would occasionally catch a glimpse of his father and Peter cursing another ugly loss. Bill's withdrawal did not go unnoticed. Sassone dubbed him "the most reclusive [owner] in Chicago sports." On the rare occasion when he did make a public statement, his comments were usually prefaced by "in a rare interview."

The substance of such remarks may have held within them a clue to Bill's reclusiveness. During the 1997–98 season, for example, he slammed GM Bob Murray, who had come in for stiff criticism from reporters and fans for that season's flop. In the same interview, however, he also defended Murray, accusing the league of infecting the Hawks with a sort of virus of uninspired play. "Bizarre," Sassone called the remark. "It's no wonder the franchise is in a downward spiral so severe that it may take years to recover."

Bill's reputation as a skinflint, meanwhile, once the type of fan lament that was easily dismissed as typical grousing, hardened into an unshakable indictment immortalized by *Tribune* columnist Bob Verdi's damning two-word nickname: Dollar Bill.

The team's accelerating decline came as Bill pushed for the putting out to pasture of perhaps the most nostalgically potent symbol of the good ol' days, the lone aspect of the franchise for which the fans professed continued and unconditional love: the quirky, raucous, deeply beloved Madhouse on Madison.

Venerated as it was, as closely associated with the lunch pail ethos of the Blackhawks and their fans, the great gray Stadium, with its leaky locker rooms and lack of amenities, was no longer viable in the luxury-box world of buildings rising in state-of-the-art splendor in big cities across the country.

As wistfully as they considered the idea of replacing such a monument, fans also demanded much more in the way of game-day experience—big screens, larger capacity, better bathrooms, improved concessions. The best players, meanwhile, signed with teams that, unlike the Blackhawks, didn't force them to clomp up stairs in their skates just to reach the ice and offered facilities that didn't look like they were built in Babe Ruth's day.

Team owners realized that they could no longer compete financially with franchises that could entertain corporate bigwigs in skybox suites leased for millions, offer arenas that could pack in several thousand more fans, and provide craft beers and brisket sandwiches along with the regular hotdog and pretzel fare. What's more, in a new trend toward corporate naming rights, they were missing out on tens of millions by playing in outdated stadiums. United Airlines, in this case, ponied up tens of millions for the privilege of dubbing the new venue that would replace the Stadium as the United Center.

Bill rightly recognized all of this—as did United Center co-owner Jerry Reinsdorf, whose Michael Jordan–led Bulls were one of the most famous teams in the world at the time—and as the '90s dawned Bill made the building of a new stadium his legacy.

If the idea was sound, the timing was awful. Instead of coming off as a forward-looking visionary, Bill was excoriated as a greedy owner bent on robbing the city and its fans of a cherished landmark to further line his pockets. That the new building would shove aside lifelong residents of the surrounding impoverished neighborhoods further cast Bill as a sort of Simon LeGree.

Protests arose and the people of the Near West Side, not yet gentrified as it would be in later years, packed hearings. At one such meeting, Rocky was called to represent the project only to have a particularly angry resident wave a gun. Rocky, acting as if it were a perfectly reasonable way to express disagreement, forged ahead and answered every question.

And anyway, once set into motion, the replacing of the old with the new was all but a fait accompli. So it was on a raw February morning in 1995 that about a hundred mourners gathered at 1800 West Madison to watch the first wrecking ball slam into the ribs of the Stadium. Officials tried to spin the demolition as a celebration of better things to come. In reality, it was more like a wake for better things gone by. The city's newspapers conveyed the tone through a variety of metaphors. "The majestic and tired Chicago Stadium took a blow harder than Jack Dempsey ever shot to the abdomen," *Sun-Times* reporter Lori Rotenberk wrote. Some onlookers booed. One bystander, Joe Rodriguez, using his hands to shield his two-year-old son from the dust, murmured "there goes history."

Even Bill, who almost by force of will had brought the city to this moment, wept as the wrecking ball remorselessly carried on its pitiless work, the spectacle the more poignant for the newer, shinier model's foundation awaiting its ribbon cutting across the street. "I came here as a boy," Bill, now a tired-looking sixty-five, mused as he watched. "My father saved that building. . . . It's a sad day, but economically it had to be done."

Indeed, the new arena would be physically better in every way than the old. At a cost of $175 million, the facility would be able to fit nearly five thousand more fans into Blackhawks games and boast more than two hundred luxury suites. More importantly at the time, it could accommodate two thousand more basketball fans, an important factor for Jerry Reinsdorf, a fifty-fifty partner in the newly formed United Center Joint Venture group that would operate the center. After a tussle with the city, it would even eschew the use of public funds, financing the project through a banking syndicate involving Japan, Australia, and France.

• • •

If Bill had nourished a feisty relationship with fans before (Gil Stein, a longtime NHL executive, claimed he once heard Bill say, "Every time Chicago fans boo me, I raise their ticket prices"), his prickliness only grew as the team settled into its new digs. Fans raged over everything from the trading away of favorites such as Jeremy Roenick and Chris Chelios to the perennial gripe about the failure to televise home games to the gripe that the new stadium was cold, sterile, and lacked the mystique of the old Stadium. "After 1996, I said I would never set foot in the building," Blackhawks fan Jeff Evans wrote on the *Daily Herald's* letters page. "I went back once last year and again this year, [but] I will never attend another game as long as the team is owned by Bill Wirtz or the family. They've finally beaten the hockey fan out of me."

"How long does Bill Wirtz . . . expect fans to wait for evidence of progress?" wondered Erick Eck, another fan writing to the *Herald*. "Are fans supposed to wait another 10 years for a competitive hockey team? Isn't [the lousy] attendance at the UC getting through to Wirtz?"

Indeed, the team's home attendance had begun to plummet in what became another ignominious streak: a dozen years of drops (with one exception), from a high of an average of 20,390 fans per game in 1995 to 12,700 in 2007, the second worst in the league.

As for who bore responsibility, a sampling of headlines tells the story:

Blame Rests in Hawks' Front Office
Wirtz Blew It With Hull—So What Else Is New?
Wirtz Owes the Fans Some Sort of Explanation
The Wirtz Curse: Why Chicago Fans Trash Blackhawks

"Some of the stuff was really cutting," Rocky recalls—nowhere more than on the Internet, which brimmed with blogs such as wirtzsucks.com and killbillwirtz.blogspot.com.

Salting the wound in liberal doses was the coincidental success of Chicago's other hockey team, the minor league Chicago Wolves. Owned by Chicago businessmen Don Levin and Buddy Meyers, the American Hockey League club was averaging almost eight thousand a night in home attendance at Allstate Arena in Rosemont. Many observers read the Wolves' ad campaign as a veiled slap at the Blackhawks. "We Play Hockey the Old-Fashioned Way," the slogan said. "We Actually Win."

To have a minor league hockey team from the same city tweaking an Original Six franchise in this way was mortifying, but the first decade of the twenty-first century brought little ammunition with which to fight back.

Then, on December 15, 2003, came a tragedy so shocking that it momentarily distracted from all other woes. Keith Magnuson, a fiery redhead who played all 589 games of his ten-year NHL career as a defenseman for the Blackhawks, died in a car crash outside of Toronto. His ferocious, high energy embodied everything Hawks fans loved about hockey, and indeed his play had made him one of the club's all-time fan favorites.

Bill's reaction ranks among his finest moments as an owner and a human being. "He dropped everything, as if mourning over a blood relative," Bob Verdi, who was often critical of Bill, wrote in a moving column for the *Tribune*. He reached out to the defenseman's family and brought the body back to Chicago, Magnuson's adopted hometown. He arranged the funeral and paid for all expenses—"a gesture that seemed to outsiders so uncharacteristic of a fabulously wealthy individual often portrayed as cold, heartless and possessed by squeezing a penny until it grew into a dime," Verdi wrote.

Bill's generosity wasn't enough to overcome the continued criticism of his leadership of the Hawks, however. A week after Magnuson's death, Sassone wrote that the outpouring for the player "underscored one thing: Hockey and the Hawks used to be big in this town. Real big." Now, he continued, "the cold and sterile United Center is half empty on most nights. There hasn't been a legitimate star player for the Hawks since Chris Chelios left."

Sassone did not stop there: "This is a hockey town, and it's filled with people who want to be Hawks fans again. Bill Wirtz speaks of how great a role model Magnuson was. How about re-stocking the team with more people like him?"

Bill's humiliation was made complete the following year when ESPN named the once-mighty Blackhawks not merely the worst franchise in hockey, but in all of pro sports. Then, for good measure, the network named Bill one of its greediest owners. "From bad to Wirtz," opened the article announcing the mortifying achievements. " 'Sad?' It's not sad. It *used* to be sad. Nobody cares enough to be sad anymore. Other NHL franchises are poorly run. But for consistently gruesome seasons, the Chicago Blackhawks are a tough act to follow."

• • •

Rocky watched it all, hurt by the constant beating the family name was taking and frustrated at his inability to do anything about it. "I couldn't understand it," Rocky says of his father. "He had been a superb businessman for so long, and other stuff wasn't this way, but he developed a blind spot when it came to the Blackhawks."

Frugality, for example, was fine as far as it went, but the team was not going to penny-pinch its way back to success—the lone business strategy that seemed to Bill worthwhile or that he was willing to pursue. Exhibit A was the ban on televising home games. The reality, as Rocky and most everyone could see, was that TV *increased* profits through lucrative television contracts and by raising awareness of the brand—to say nothing of the goodwill such a gesture would have demonstrated to fans.

Meanwhile, while those millions sat like an unclaimed pot of gold, Bill obsessed over quarters in the couch. For example, though peanut vendors had prowled the sidewalks for years in front of Chicago Stadium, Bill banned them from outside the United Center because fans weren't allowed to bring in outside food. The decision set off a silly spat that only reinforced Bill's reputation as a skinflint and, worse, stole his time and attention away from issues that actually mattered, such as marketing and advertising. He also went after Mark Weinberg, a lawyer who for years published *Blue Line*, a crude, profane unofficial program that routinely lampooned Bill and his handling of the team in the most vulgar ways possible. Rather than do the smart thing and ignore it, Bill punched back, at times with somewhat shocking force. In January 2001, for example, two United Center security guards tackled Weinberg, pulled him to the ground, then had him arrested. "They say I took a swing at them," Weinberg told the *Chicago Reader*. "That's so absurd I'm almost amazed they're even saying it."

It was not the first time Weinberg had been arrested while trying to sell his programs. A decade earlier, a week after the first issue, Chicago police approached him on a sidewalk before a Hawks game and hauled him to jail for obstructing pedestrian traffic. Weinberg accused Bill of being behind the move and the charges were dropped, but the feud continued unabated and, if anything, grew more heated.

Weinberg dragged Bill into court, suing him over locker room access and his war on the outside peanut vendors. Those cases were ultimately dismissed, but not before Bill was forced to bring in a fleet of presumably high-priced attorneys at a cost that exceeded by magnitude the few dollars he might have lost to some poor neighborhood residents trying to make a few bucks. The cost of the negative publicity generated was incalculable.

The ludicrousness of Bill's pettiness did not end there. Rocky perceived in his father "almost a kind of jealousy that players were making so much more money than many of the front office guys. It was like, 'They're driving around in Cadillacs' and he'd be damned if he was going to coddle them any further." Such an attitude made no sense to Rocky. "Well, so what [if they have nice cars]?" he says. "How they spend their money is their business."

What his father failed to notice is that luring the best players often takes providing some perks. Savvy owners realized this and made big investments in amenities such as big, comfortable locker rooms and state-of-the-art training facilities that would make big-name free agents *want* to play for them. Bill flatly refused even the barest of incentives. One example was travel. Virtually every other NHL club paid for charter flights for away games, if not a team-owned jet—an accommodation that was more practical than pampering. If a game went late—into double or triple overtime, say—exhausted players would not have to fight their way through the airport and cram onto commercial flights. They also would not have to deal with petty delays, worry about their baggage, or contend with any of the other annoyances that come with normal flights.

Bill saw it differently. "His feeling was, 'Why charter a flight? We're treating the players too well, we're being too good to them,'" Rocky says. Actually, the team was putting itself at a gross disadvantage. "The reason Detroit does so well is precisely *because* they treat their players very well," says Rocky. "It's an investment."

For Hawks fans, Bill's attitude was an indictment: they were living and dying with their team, while Bill was counting paper clips and fuming over the money he was losing to neighborhood guys trying to scrape a few bucks selling peanuts.

Bill's supporters, including perhaps his biggest cheerleader, Peter, denied that Bill was cheap or that his personal resentments got in the way of him wanting to build a winner. Rocky himself acknowledges that Bill loved the sport and wanted badly to win, but also that his personal emotions clouded his judgment in ways detrimental to the team's success.

It confounded Rocky, meanwhile, that the front office seemed nonchalant about the team's mediocrity. "There was no urgency," Rocky says. "There was nothing. Not even saying something as simple as, 'Our goal is to win the Stanley Cup.'"

To Rocky, that lack of a simple, clear mission statement was unfathomable, bizarre even. "You're in a sport where the Holy Grail is that singular pursuit," he says. "And yet, they would never say it."

Instead, per Peter, the 2002 slogan was "Restore the Roar." Later, it was "Red Rising."

Meanwhile, rather than investing in scouting and farm clubs to build a team people would want to see, the front office relied on gimmicks such as dropping ticket prices and having players (to their embarrassment) hand out business cards around town that fans could cash in for free seats.

Even then Rocky believed he could step in and make an immediate difference. His mind was full of ideas, in fact, but even though he was an officer of the team, no one was asking. Not Bill certainly, and if not Bill, then not Peter, now senior vice president of the Blackhawks. In fact, by 2005 or so, Rocky had the growing sense that his father and brother were actively working to find a way to keep Rocky from ever taking over the team, perhaps finding a loophole in the family succession plan that would allow Peter to be installed as club president, while cutting Rocky out of anything to do with the team.

As it was, Rocky had already been effectively excommunicated by Bill when it came to anything involving the Blackhawks. In what surely was no oversight, Rocky wasn't even included in the team's media guide, despite being a vice president and an alternate governor to the NHL board.

In one sense, unwitting as it might have been, his father and brother were doing Rocky a favor. If you're shut out of decision-making, you're also not to blame. Thus, when fans, friends, or associates would ask what was wrong with the Hawks, he could merely shrug and rightly say he didn't understand the strategy, or lack of it, either.

Rocky's relative anonymity provided another advantage. At games, he could walk the concourses unrecognized and simply observe what was working and what wasn't. He could listen to the fans' complaints in all their raw fury, without filters. That's not to say that his low profile was always pleasant. The team's vice president of marketing at the time treated Rocky with barely masked contempt ("I didn't exist," as Rocky puts it), either forgetting or not caring that the man he was disrespecting could one day have the power to fire him. (Which, in fact, was what happened. "One of my first moves," Rocky says.)

To further alienate him from the team, meanwhile, his father "would do this divide and conquer stuff, where he'd communicate his anger through other people." When Bill wanted to seriously discuss something, for example, he and Peter would either hole themselves up in Bill's office at the United Center or confab in a small private room off the Sonja Henie lounge just off of gate 119. "It was all dysfunctional communication," Rocky says.

The reality was that "I was involved in all the businesses," says Rocky, including, though tangentially, the Blackhawks. With the franchise, in fact, he played a far more important role than anyone realized—or that Bill acknowledged: "We still had to raise money for Wirtz Corp. to cover the losses of the Hawks."

In public, Bill and Peter seemed bent on portraying Peter as the inevitable Hawks president, ignoring the plan of succession that would leave any such decision in Rocky's hands. "He thought he would be president," Rocky says. "He thought Dad could appoint him."

Whenever he was asked about his father, Peter would defend him. "I love my father and would step in front of a car for him if I had to," Peter told the *Tribune's* Terry Armour in 2002. "The people who know my father know that he's a very genuine, caring individual. His public persona is so different from how he really is."

When asked about being the heir apparent to run the team, Peter played coy. "It's never really discussed," Peter told the *Sun-Times* in 1995. "I love the Blackhawks and always want to be involved . . . but as far as the future goes, we really don't talk about it." Two years later, when the paper indicated that Peter would likely take over, he again demurred. "My father has always been proud of the strength and integrity of our logo," he said, "and I would do anything to maintain that." He added, "But I can't predict the future."

Rocky would read such comments with a mixture of bemusement and, in the case of the family's alleged silence over the succession issue, with astonishment. "That is the one thing we *did* talk about," Rocky says. "It's the *only* thing we talked about. We talked about it forever."

And forever, the bottom line remained inescapable. After Michael (now gone), Arthur's plan placed Rocky as the next head of the family business. No exceptions. Full stop.

Nevertheless, Rocky says, Peter and Bill continued to search for any hint of an escape clause. According to Rocky, for example, after Bill died, Peter asked his assistant, Cindy, "is there anything in Dad's will that talks about me inheriting the Blackhawks?"

The answer was no, but even if it had been yes, such a bequeathal would have been meaningless because "Dad didn't own the Blackhawks, the company did," Rocky says. For Peter to even ask the question "shows you the level of delusion," Rocky adds.

Apart from the will, Bill worked against Rocky on two other fronts. First, he tried to persuade Rocky to resign from Wirtz Corp. "He would write me a letter and say, 'If you want to resign, you can, I'll accept it,'" Rocky says. Bill's thinking, Rocky speculates, was that if he—Rocky—voluntarily stepped down from Wirtz Corp. he also would be ceding his place in the line of succession. Peter would then leapfrog Rocky and become the heir. Once again, whether Rocky resigned and flew to Morocco to spend his days being fanned by palm leaves was utterly irrelevant. He was, as galling as it was to Bill and Peter, next in line.

In what is an interesting insight—and perhaps the key to the mystery of why Bill so forsook his eldest begotten son—Rocky theorizes that it was never he whom Bill truly resented. It was Bill's own father, Arthur. "What really pissed my Dad off was that my grandfather was still ruling him from the grave. My father was not in control and it infuriated him."

Thus did Bill open his second front in the war against his son: undermining him—smearing is not too strong a word—with the rest of the family. Gossip, rumors, and outright lies constituted Bill's arsenal. "He would try to sour people about me by saying things that weren't true, just to make me look bad to them," Rocky says. In that sense, says Rocky, it's understandable that they would regard him with something less than sibling affection. "He never said anything good to the siblings about me, so what are they going to think?" he says. "He told them lies about me and my behavior."

Bruce Wirtz MacArthur, president of the family's First National Bank of South Miami in Florida, recalls but one example. Bill, he says, was musing one day about the succession plan over a glass of Scotch after the death of his brother, Michael. Out of the blue—or what seemed to be to Bruce—Bill abruptly warned that Rocky had been planning to fire him when he took over. MacArthur was stunned. "It hit me like a ton of bricks. I thought, 'what did I do to Rocky?' " Having little reason to believe Bill was lying to him, MacArthur lived the next several years under a cloud, wondering how he had offended his cousin so badly that he would fire his own kin. "I started saving like a squirrel going into a long winter," MacArthur says. "I put away every dime I could because that's what I thought was going to happen."

Rocky, oblivious to any of it at the time, now confirms the story. He learned about it, in fact, from MacArthur himself. "I didn't know about it until after Dad had died, and Bruce confronted me at Dad's wake," Rocky says. As stunned as MacArthur was, Rocky assured him that he had never contemplated any such thing. If anything,

Rocky says, Bill himself seemed to have it in for Bruce. "Dad would hammer him," Rocky recalls. "Just verbally hammer him. I'd say, 'Bruce, if you stay away from him, he can't do that stuff to you,' " but that was easier said than done.

"Cruelty is unchecked anger," Rocky says. "And Dad could be very cruel at certain times. And he was very cruel to Bruce in my opinion."

Rocky endured similar abuse from his father, but rather than let it wound him, he learned to play rope-a-dope, a technique used by Muhammad Ali that lured an opponent into punching himself out. "I felt like my job was to be like a club boxer," Rocky says. "A club boxer is someone who has to go twelve rounds and duke it out and stand up to the end to get paid. That was my job. Take it. You were never gonna win, but just stand there and just be there. No matter how many head shots you took, you've still got to be standing."

Rocky later learned that Peter took his own shots, primarily in the form of a whisper campaign with both his siblings and with Bill's sister, Betty. "He would tell them that I couldn't be trusted," Rocky says.

Just how potent the campaign was became clear one day when Rocky spied a document Bill had not-so-subtly left on his desk: Betty's will. "I looked at it and realized that everyone's name was in it in some form or another—except mine." Having assumed he had a good relationship with his aunt, Rocky reached out. "I said, 'You know, what you do with your will is your business, but I'd at least like to be named to have some involvement as your trustee, so it's not just Peter and Arthur.' "

Rocky's call confirmed a growing sense with Betty that something was amiss. The Rocky being described to her by Peter and his siblings wasn't the Rocky she knew. "I thought, there's something wrong with this picture," she told me over lunch in Springfield, Illinois, where she lives a relatively modest life, but still follows her family's fortunes. "Peter would call me and say this and that" about Rocky, she recalls. "I'd listen, and I really tried to not be judgmental, but I thought this is bad." Betty says Rocky's other siblings called her, too, and spoke negatively about their brother. "I was very much being coerced by Rocky's siblings to go to Peter's side. I guess, as they say, when people die and money is involved, things really can change."

Betty met with her nephew in Chicago while in town for a doctor's appointment. She acknowledged the calls, but had no idea Bill was involved too. When Rocky detailed what was happening, she says the revelation was stunning. "It was really difficult."

Something else struck her: that while Rocky's siblings were bad-mouthing him to her, Rocky had never done anything remotely the same. Years later, when Rocky took over and Peter quit the Blackhawks, "Rocky was actually worried about him," Betty says. "Rocky probably wouldn't admit it today, but he called me after he'd gotten Peter's email on the heels of Bill passing away. And Rocky was concerned about him. He was not as angry as he was concerned."

After talking with Rocky and others, Betty did a complete about-face, removing Peter as a trustee. What's more, when the family attorney, Gene Gozdecki, offered to break the news to Peter, she refused. "I said I'll tell him," she says.

What still angers Betty, nearly as much as the backstabbing, is what she sees as an astonishing lack of gratitude for what he eventually accomplished: an elevation of the company that benefitted them both financially and—through restoration of the family name—personally. "If it were me, I'd be encouraging him to eat right, asking just what can I do for you? Because, he turned it around, he made some tough decisions—things are good.

"I am very thrilled, I am honored to be his aunt. I hope the siblings will be nice to him. He works so hard, he gives them so much money and their stock is worth so much more now."

• • •

There were bright spots. One shined down while Rocky was at the Ocean Reef Club in Florida for an industry function, and a mutual friend introduced him to a woman from Columbus, Ohio, named Marilyn Queen, who was vacationing in the resort town. Outgoing, fun, bold, brassy, Marilyn was a dynamo. She had previously owned a restaurant, but having sold it was bartending at the time she met Rocky. Other than their immediate and undeniable compatibility, two things struck Rocky: One was her utter lack of pretension. "She had no airs about who you were or what you did," Rocky says. And two, "She had no idea who I was," he says. "She couldn't care less about social status." When someone told her that his family owned the Blackhawks, she shrugged. "Oh? That's nice."

He also admired her devotion to her daughter, who was in the sixth grade at the time. "She would always put her daughter before herself," he says. "Anything to make life better for her."

With all that he was going through with his own family, with his marriage on the rocks, Rocky was deeply grateful for Marilyn's support and even more so for her presence. Her exuberance was both refreshing and contagious—exactly what Rocky needed in the midst of so much family turmoil.

The other promising development for Rocky in those years was the maturation of his son, Danny. The youth had grown from a buttoned-up mirror of a teenage Rocky into a hipster who favored piercings and dyed hair into a successful player in music promotion and advertising. He'd gained a keen understanding of the lightning expansion of digital video, audio, and social media. "Growing up, I was a preppy kid who went to Loyola and parted my hair the same as my Dad," Danny says with a laugh. "Out in the world, I was expressing myself a little more in terms of how I looked. My hair changed colors a few times."

Unlike Rocky, Danny played hockey when he was a kid. "I loved the sport," he says. He played for Loyola Academy, a powerhouse at the time. In his senior year, the team won the state championship. He chose Boston College in large part because of its excellent hockey program—an amenity he could now enjoy as a spectator rather than a player.

For a time, he interned at Hawk Quarters, the Michigan Avenue merchandise store run by Uncle Pete, but he also had internships at major record labels. "I was committed to learning the music business," he says. "I promoted concerts, records—I had listening parties. At the time, I saw it as my career path, though in the back of my mind I always had a desire to connect it back to the family business."

For his part, Rocky hoped very much that his son would one day become involved with Wirtz Corp., but he was equally committed to letting Danny find his own way, in both business and life. "It was—what can I do to help Danny be a better businessman and not tell him how to do it, but to give him support?" Rocky says. "With me, growing up, it was: Dad or Grandpa made the decision and now you go along with it."

Rocky, for example, kept mum on the colored hair. "I would come home for Christmas with bright red spiky hair or bright platinum blonde hair, and, to be honest with you, he got over that pretty easily," Danny says. But even Rocky had limits. In Danny's case, it was when he got a tongue piercing.

"I told him that if I see it, your car is coming home on a flatbed truck," Rocky says.

Still, Danny was grateful. "People talk today about how Rocky can get along with anybody and that his biggest strength is relationship building," Danny says. "It showed in our relationship just how open he can be."

When Danny told his father he wanted to explore the music industry rather than join the family business—which, as the oldest son of the owner, he would have a claim to running one day—Rocky couldn't have been more supportive, Danny says. He found work at a music company in New York that expanded into brand marketing and worked on a campaign for Smirnoff vodka. "I was like, 'Dad, do we sell Smirnoff?' He said, 'Danny, that's the number one brand in the state of Illinois. We sell a lot of Smirnoff.' The worlds were connecting a little bit."

He met his soon-to-be-wife Anne, who worked in digital marketing, in New York. As much as they loved life in the Big Apple, the couple jumped at a chance to move to the fashionable East End of London for a year. There, Danny worked with some of the top names in the industry, including Mick Rock, the photographer who shot David Bowie and other rock legends.

By 2006, however, he felt a tug back to the Midwest. "I was getting older and just thinking, 'Where am I going? What am I doing?' I had something calling me back to the family business, back home to Chicago, maybe starting a new business and having it operate under Wirtz Corp. I had this feeling in my heart that it was going to happen, and maybe soon, but I just wasn't quite ready, not yet." As fate would have it, the London firm he worked for closed shop. "And then, my grandpa began to get sick."

• • •

Bill's behavior continued to deteriorate to the point that some acquaintances worried that something more serious was going on than the strokes and other health issues. He seemed to be showing signs of dementia. Rocky was first alerted to the symptoms by Peter's longtime girlfriend. "She told me, 'You know, your father's acting kind of funny,'" Rocky recalls. "Sometimes he forgets things."

Bill's assistant noticed similar problems. "She told me he was getting lost while driving sometimes," Rocky says. "Dad knew the city really well, well enough to be a taxi driver, but he was getting disoriented." Once, on the way to a corporate board meeting in downtown Chicago, Bill phoned his friend and fellow member John Miller to say he was having trouble finding the location. Miller asked where he was. "Aurora," he answered—a suburban city more than forty miles away.

In another troubling incident, he accused his sister Betty of spreading gossip about him. "He was always so sweet and loving toward me," she says. "I had never seen him act that way." Betty racked her brain to come up with anything she might have said. Perhaps something was misinterpreted. She eventually wrote him a letter assuring him that she would never do such a thing—but by then he'd forgotten all about it.

Alarmed, Rocky asked Peter if he thought their father might be showing early signs of dementia. "I reached out because I wanted to try to get him help," Rocky says. Days later, Rocky received a searing phone call from his father, railing at him for daring to suggest he was failing, the implication being that Rocky was trying to pull off some kind of coup. The unhinged response by Bill shocked even Rocky. "It was out of the ordinary even for him," Rocky says. "So I called Peter up and said, 'Did you happen to share our conversation about dementia with Dad?' And he said, 'I felt I had to.'"

Rocky was shocked. Peter knew how sensitive their father was to suggestions that he might be mentally impaired. Given that, Rocky just assumed that Peter would keep the conversation between them. When his brother admitted he had shared the private chat, "I thought, how can one brother stoop so low, brother to brother. How can he betray the confidence of his brother like that, knowing that it would start World War III with their father?"

Sure enough, Rocky listened as his father raged at him over the phone for more than an hour, a confused tantrum filled with wild conspiracy theories and disconnected thoughts during which Bill rained blow after blow on his elder son, unleashing emotional haymakers that seemed thrown through decades of resentment and long-forgotten ancient grievances. Rocky took it, including Bill's bellowing demand that he quit the company, give up his claim to the chairmanship, his claim to everything, including and especially his involvement with the Blackhawks.

As deeply wounded as Rocky was, he forced himself to find empathy for the outburst. His father wasn't in his right mind, Rocky believed, and he found it deeply sad to see what his Dad had become, in part through no fault of his own: a bitter, cruel man who saw conspiracies around every corner and who clung to grudges and anger against a son who would have given most anything to return to the days when his father brought him along to hockey games and cracked his friends up in living room sessions with Joan by his side. Those days were gone, Rocky knew, never to return, and the accompanying realization hurt as much as any fit of pique. In the end, his father was far more easy to love than to like. When it came to Peter, however, Rocky could summon no such compassion, no such warm feelings. Since the day Rocky confronted him over his girlfriend, the two had achieved a sort of détente. A Blackhawks publicity still—maybe one of the only official photos extant of the father and brothers together—belies the long-simmering tension. The three men, standing on the ice, the dark, empty stands just visible behind them, pose in crisp white dress shirts, arms at their sides. Bill, in the middle, his once-dark hair now handsomely silvered, wears a broad smile as warm and sincere as perhaps any image ever captured of him, his eyes crinkled, deep creases bracketing a toothy, full-on grin. Tellingly, Peter, wearing a mustache and looking typically trim, stands to his right. He also wears a tie that, like his father's, is light blue; Rocky's is red. And even though the elder son stands slightly closer to his father, both his carriage and expression are subtly suggestive of apartness, not quite remote, but not quite affectionate, the distance, if not from his father, then certainly from Peter. For unlike

Rocky's view toward his dad—one of compassion and empathy—his feelings toward Peter remained as cold as the ice they stood on that day, a sense of bad blood that by all accounts was then, and remains still, mutual.

The Passing of Dollar Bill

In the final, doleful months of Bill Wirtz's life, the negative headlines, the withering criticism, the sometimes violent tantrums by Bill and the sometimes personal attacks by the newspapers, the unchecked free fall of the Blackhawks, and the professional exile of Rocky, all continued apace and unabated. Bill's growing health problems—the most serious of which was silently and rapidly metastasizing—undoubtedly contributed to the shuddersome confluence of events.

That spring of 2007, the annual postmortem on the Blackhawks played like a dirge, fitting for a team that finished last in the Central Division, behind even the expansion Columbus Blue Jackets. "This has become a national joke," the *Daily Herald* sighed, in a three-part series devoted to the team's slow-motion demise, aptly titled "Glory Days to Meltdown." Indeed, the paper wrote, "Only standups could dream up this material."

The *Sun-Times*, no less exasperated, chimed in with a different analogy: "You know the saying if a tree falls in the woods but no one is there to hear it, does it make a sound?" the writer asked. "With the Hawks, is it [even] worth yelling, 'Timber'?"

Wisecracks like that, cutting as they were, drew inspiration from more than the team's embarrassing record. A variety of gimmicky promotions, each of which died aborning, elicited rueful chuckles. One in particular seemed to capture the futility of the franchise. Hoping to lure fans back to the United Center, the team offered hundreds of free and heavily discounted tickets to "lucky winners" of a contest, a giveaway that turned into yet more black humor when the seats went unclaimed. One fan spoke for many in explaining the debacle: "You can't expect people to come out and watch this," he told the *Daily Herald*—even for free.

Among the most damning factors in the Hawks' ongoing struggles was the front office penchant for changing coaches, general managers, or both almost as often as the earth circled the sun. Despite his reputation and Dollar Bill nickname, Bill spent more than the fans gave him credit for. But even then, the money always went, it seemed, to the wrong player at the wrong time—a big name who was washed up, a free agent who never lived up to his contract, a new coach just as the old one was gaining a little traction. In 2006, for example, general manager Bob Pulford lavished a four-year, $16 million deal on Adrian Aucoin, a once productive defenseman whom the front office felt had a few good years left. But in the single season he played for the Hawks, Aucoin struggled with injuries and steadily lost playing time before waiving his deal and moving on.

Compounding problems, Bill failed to pony up when it came to keeping players who *were* worth the heavier price, if only to mollify the fans who loved them. Jeremy Roenick and Chris Chelios, for example, were traded (Roenick to the Phoenix Coyotes, Chelios to the Detroit Red Wings) to avoid meeting their free agent demands. Roenick notched two seasons as the Coyotes' leading scorer and played in two all-star games; Chelios, admittedly long in the tooth at thirty-seven, earned first-team all-star honors in his first year with the Red Wings and played an instrumental role in the club's successful Stanley Cup run.

To be fair, flops happen. Traded players sometimes make you pay dearly for letting them go. Draft picks—even "sure things"—fail to fulfill expectations. All of those things can be forgiven if the team has done its due diligence in vetting and assessment. In the case of the Blackhawks, however, that was not the case. Decisions were made on the word of other league executives, past histories, or gut feelings. All of those have a place, but in the modern age of sabermetrics—which allows a granular, empirical analysis of most every aspect of a player and his potential—as well as sophisticated psychological and medical profiling, they amount to a dart tossed with closed eyes at a very tiny bull's-eye. Other teams saw that reality and embraced it. Bill, stubborn to the end, dismissed such tools as newfangled gimmickry that barely considered the quality he valued above all others: personal loyalty.

Nowhere was that ethos more on display than in Bill's approach to the front office—specifically, coaches and general managers. With no other aspect of the franchise was he less willing to pay big bucks. Indeed, when it came to hiring coaches, Bill not only lived up to his Dollar Bill nickname, he enshrined it in amber. "He just didn't feel like coaches were worth big salaries," Rocky says.

As with players, he also shunned the kind of in-depth candidate analysis that is considered essential today when it came to picking coaches. The seeming caprice was one of the first things John McDonough noticed when he took over and remains one of the most puzzling. "When you have, in a ten-year period, five general managers and seven or eight head coaches," says McDonough, "it sort of says it all. How are you getting to the promised land when every seventeen months you're changing personnel, systems, coaches?"

As ever, Bill took the heaviest fire. But, now that he was seventy-seven, the character of the criticism changed. Scribes still delighted in bad-pun headlines—"Wirtz-Case Scenario for Hawks" was the groaner over an April 12 *Sun-Times* column—but more and more he was belittled as the "Old Man," out of touch and more worthy of pity than panning. "There's no use being upset with him anymore," Greg Couch wrote. "His story has simply become sad. . . . The image now is of an old man with failing health and cloudy thoughts sitting in an empty stadium insisting that his way is the right way."

Bill continued to slug back—mostly through letters and faxes now. He continued trying to impose his will on the league and anything or anyone else within his orbit, though having stepped down as chairman of the Board of Governors in 1992, his bite was, anymore, mostly toothless. That did not stop him from still throwing the occasional haymaker. In a rare interview—given to the *Toronto Star* rather than a Chicago paper—Bill threatened to sell the team if the NHL Players Association installed a labor hard-liner as the new executive director. Whether that was the deciding factor, Bill got his way.

The threat itself, however, inspired a fresh round of media jabs. The *Daily Herald* responded, "Oh, if only." Columnist Barry Rozner wrote, "Blackhawks fans are lined up around the block for the chance to drive the whole group of you to the airport—which marks the first time they've lined up for anything hockey related at the UC since Moses was in high school."

While Bill either laughed off or punched back at such criticisms, the family suffered. "It was very, very hard," Betty Wirtz says. "Bill was always charming to me, always wonderful," but the press portrayed him as anything but.

As the last days of that summer dwindled, however, the family fretted over more than bad headlines. Namely, they were worried about Bill's increasingly disturbing behavior. Still driving his big black Cadillac, he was getting lost regularly now. One person close to the family dropped by the Wirtz house in the morning to pay a quick visit that turned into six hours of awkwardness. Several times Bill burned an attempt to make breakfast for the two. At one point, the visitor overheard him trying to buy shares in Walmart for the sole purpose of protesting plans by the retailing giant to put a store across from the family farm in Fremont, outside of Wauconda, Illinois.

On another occasion, that same friend ran into Bill pushing one cart and pulling another through a Bed Bath & Beyond store. "The carts were packed with stuff—two of everything." When the friend mentioned it to Bill's wife, Ittie, he recalls her telling him, "Oh, yeah. It makes him feel good. I wind up taking everything back."

The family did its best to shield Bill's deteriorating condition from the public eye, but the situation was becoming untenable. Bill's tantrum against Rocky alone raised serious questions regarding dementia.

Bill was nevertheless still boss when he was hospitalized for urinary tract problems in August 2007. Tests uncovered the presence of something potentially more serious: cancer cells in his bladder. An operation to remove the organ confirmed it. "As soon as it was taken out, the doctors realized that the cancer had spread to his lungs," Rocky says. The prognosis was brutal. Without chemotherapy or radiation, Bill had a few weeks, maybe a month, to live. Bill was stubborn to the end: he underwent chemo, but too late to have much effect. Unspoken was a deadly reality: Bill was past saving.

He continued to run the company on the phone in his last days, receiving visitors in the hospital when he felt up to it. He also continued to seek ways to somehow circumvent his own father's succession plan and install Peter as head of the Blackhawks.

The public knew nothing about the seriousness of Bill's illness and certainly not Bill's machinations regarding his elder son.

Rocky knew and struggled with his feelings toward his father. He had always acknowledged Bill's brilliance and, despite their clashes and what can accurately be called cruelty from his Dad, had remained loyal.

Just when their relationship had reached its nadir, however, a flash of light broke through. Both brothers were in Bill's room. By this point, Rocky says, his father had made peace with his condition. "He knew he wasn't coming out of the hospital." That day dawned sunny, clear, and warm and now, with his sons by his side, he looked out the window at the trees and sun and the birds. Never a reflective man, rarely even mellow—at least that he let on—Bill seemed suddenly overtaken. His eyes grew misty as he continued to gaze at the life playing out just beyond the walls of his own shrunken world. "He just said, 'Everyone should go through something like this, an experience like this,'" Rocky recalls. "'It is a humbling thing.'"

Looking back so many years later, Rocky believes his father realized, as if for the first time, that he wasn't in control—perhaps never was when it came to the broader questions of life—and never would be again. Through his tears, Rocky says, "he was conveying that idea that, 'Death is a humbling experience.'"

To Rocky, the moment represented the kind of remarkable, if heartbreaking, flash of insight that for some sadly comes only in their final hours. "Facing death squarely and being completely at ease with it," Rocky says. "Acceptance of reality and what it is to be alive and to be dying. Seeing that, feeling it deeply, and then saying, 'I accept that I have no control over my destiny.' It was such an experience for him because I don't think he ever thought he was going to die."

Rocky was moved and sad for his father. He didn't think he needed to forgive him—there was nothing, Rocky felt, that needed forgiving. The disrespect, the belittling, the excommunication—even the efforts to deny him his rightful place as heir to the Wirtz throne—those expressions of anger had been his father's to bear, had eaten at his father's soul, not Rocky's.

As Bill's days dwindled, Rocky found solace in another unexpected family development: his son, Danny, who had been living in London with his wife, Anne, decided to come home—not just to be by his grandfather's side, but permanently. Rocky had felt an inkling even before Bill's illness, but chose not to push. "My dad never called up and said, 'Danny, you better get your ass home because your grandpa's about to die,'" Danny says. "I just sort of knew that it was time." Rocky didn't pressure his son to join the family business either. "He just said, in a very noncommittal way, 'Let's take a look and see, maybe there's something at one of our beverage companies.'"

Once again, though, uplifting news seemed to come with an ugly downside. After Bill's death on September 26, Rocky wanted the world to see a side of his father that the decades of coverage had failed to capture. So, around Thanksgiving, Rocky agreed to share what transpired that day in the hospital with *Tribune* columnist Melissa Isaacson. In prose both moving and deeply sensitive, the resulting article captured the moment beautifully and in so doing paid poignant homage to a man far more complicated than the more familiar one-dimensional caricature.

A few days later, however, an email from Peter landed in Rocky's box. "He was offended that I had shared that moment," Rocky says.

Meet the New Boss

In those last days, Rocky kept the phone beside his bed in case the hospital needed to reach him with news. By then his father's condition had deteriorated to the point that the daily visits by Bill's children and his wife had become little more than a chance to sit by the dying man's bedside, stroke his hand, murmur a few words that might reach through his narcosis and provide some measure of comfort, however small.

Even so, the finality of the actual moment can never be prepared for, and when the phone rang at two in the morning on September 26, 2007, the jangle startled Rocky. A call at this hour would not be good news, and Rocky's fears were confirmed when he heard the voice on the other end of the line. Bill's private nurse said it was over. Rocky thanked her, then hung up and sat on the edge of the bed. After a few numb moments, he picked up the receiver and dialed his brother, Peter. "Dad's gone. Let's all meet at the hospital."

Within the hour, the five Wirtz siblings—Rocky, Peter, Gail, Karey, and Alison—had arrived in Evanston, where Bill had spent the final few weeks of his life in the hospice ward of the town's medical center. They gathered in a conference area, just off the corridor where his body lay under the white sheets of his private-room bed. Some wept. Peter was bereft. Eventually, they composed themselves to discuss the complexities of the arrangements that needed to be made in announcing the death: who should speak, whom to call, how they should word the statement to the press. The site of the services was not a question: Fourth Presbyterian on Michigan Avenue, the setting for most every big family event stretching back to the marriage of Arthur and Virginia.

Two days later, beginning at two on a bright autumn Sunday, a steady stream of mourners turned into a torrent at a visitation at Donnellan Funeral Home in Skokie, creating a line that stretched around the building and into the parking lot. Bill may have offended the fans, but he had touched many lives and many of those people wanted one last occasion to say farewell. The people paying their respects, including Hall of Famer Stan Mikita and boxing promoter Don King, waited an hour and a half for the opportunity to pass the casket and extend their condolences to Ittie and the siblings.

At one point, Rocky asked to speak privately to Peter and the two ducked into an adjacent flower room, where they sat opposite one another. The impromptu one-on-one was an awkward moment for reasons far beyond the setting. While they had crossed paths in recent years, most notably in the hospital room as their father lay dying, rarely had they discussed anything of substance and, indeed, each in his own way had tacitly acknowledged the deep currents of tension—the accumulated resentments of decades—coursing through even their most mundane interactions.

The intensity of that angst, Rocky knew, was only going to increase with what he was about to say. "We need to talk about the team," Rocky said. While much of the media assumed that Peter would run the franchise—understandably, given his decades in the front office—both he and Rocky knew the question had been far from decided. What they did know was that Rocky, now head of Wirtz Corp., would be the one making the call. That's what Rocky wanted to discuss, he told Peter. "The team can't keep going the way it's going," Rocky said. "We're going to need to make changes, starting with putting home games on TV."

To Rocky's relief, "he told me he was fine with that," Rocky recalls, even adding "that he would help any way he could." Then came the harder part. As for running the team, Rocky said, "until I can get my arms around what is happening, we are going to keep the presidency open." Peter, in short, would not be taking charge—then or perhaps ever. Rocky knew the words had to land like a punch, but in the moment Peter didn't show it. Instead, he nodded again and repeated his promise to help in the transition.

Unspoken was the deeper reasoning behind Rocky's decision. Peter had been so loyal to their father that Rocky assumed, rightly by most accounts, that his brother would be constitutionally incapable of reversing the core beliefs to which Bill had clung so fiercely. Given the state of the team and the dysfunction that seemed to permeate so many aspects of the franchise, however, status quo was untenable.

On a more personal level, Rocky also worried about his brother's state of mind after their father's death. More than merely sad, he was shattered, according to Rocky and his sister Gail. "He took Dad's death extremely hard," she told *Chicago* magazine in November 2008. "[Bill] was his best friend."

According to Rocky and others interviewed for this book, the relationship between Bill and Peter was even more complicated. Peter, they say, was so deferential to Bill that it crippled his own ability to be effective as an executive. "He was terrified of making a decision," Rocky says. "So he would bring Dad in on everything, including things he really shouldn't have been bothered with."

Peter, says Rocky, would go to their Dad "for 98 percent of the decisions," which meant Bill, unable to resist, would turn his entire focus to resolving the problem. As a result, Bill would become absorbed by trivial matters to the point that he began neglecting more pressing issues. For Peter, the benefit—subconscious perhaps—was the freedom from risk. "If you never make a decision then you can never be wrong and if you're never wrong you can never be yelled at," Rocky says. Peter's approach is easy to understand. He "would see me stand up to Dad about something and watch him blast me with a double-barrel shotgun," Rocky says. Peter "would sit back like, 'Oh, my God.'"

But Rocky also thinks Peter internalized one of Bill's most harmful convictions: that to disagree with him was to betray him. "Loyalty was everything to Dad," Rocky says. "You don't agree with him, it means you're not loyal to him. It didn't matter whether you were competent or not. You're loyal means you're competent." In that way, Rocky says, "Peter was Dad."

Nonetheless, Rocky thought Peter was still a valuable part of the franchise. His detailed knowledge of the books alone could provide critical information as Rocky began his audit.

A couple of days later, however, on the way home from the airport after a trip to Washington, Rocky received a call from one of the family's corporate attorneys and longtime friends, Don Hunter. "He said, 'There's a letter from Peter on your desk, but Peter wants me to explain to you what it says before you read it,'" Rocky recalls.

"Peter and I talked," the lawyer said, "and he's decided he wants to move on. He said he wanted to go and work on Bismarck [the concessions business]. He told me he wanted to write a release to the fans, and asked if I could publish that, and that he'd help me in any way in the transition."

"It hit me like a sledgehammer," Rocky recalls. "I would certainly honor his wishes, but I was bowled over. I sent an attorney to talk to him, to say, 'Why don't you sleep on it for six months?'" Rocky recalls. Peter declined.

Still dumbfounded, Rocky agreed nonetheless to grant his brother's request to publish his statement on the team website. It appeared without warning on October 5, 2007, the birthday Rocky shared with his father. The letter gushed with praise for Bill: "In addition to teaching me everything a father teaches his son about how to love, live, and give back to society, he taught me so many other lessons that I will have for the rest of my life. He was a man of his word and a man of great integrity and honor. I truly relished in being his lieutenant and felt spiritually connected to helping and supporting my father in any way I could."

And Peter included kind words for Rocky: "My brother brings with him a wealth of knowledge and enthusiasm from my family's other businesses and I know he will be successful in leading and directing the team for many years to come." Despite a pledge in the statement to give Rocky his "full cooperation and support," since then the two brothers have talked only a handful of times, with most all communications being conveyed through lawyers.

They spoke, of course, at their father's funeral, held the next day at a packed Fourth Presbyterian. In a service fitting for a head of state, the bereaved listened to Bill's old pal John Ziegler, president of the NHL during Bill's halcyon years running the Blackhawks, deliver the eulogy. Afterwards, in a consideration normally granted high government officials, the city closed streets leading westward to the United Center to make way for the funeral cortege. The hearse carrying Bill's casket drove down Madison, past the site of the old Chicago Stadium—now consigned, as he was, to history—and circled its replacement, the United Center, the building whose existence largely owed to his efforts.

One of the other rare occasions on which the brothers spoke was at the ill-fated United Center ceremony insisted on by Peter, at which their father's memory was booed.

• • •

In any case, Rocky got to work. First, he called Jerry Reinsdorf, owner of the Chicago Bulls (and White Sox) and co-owner of the United Center, a man Rocky considered a mentor. Reinsdorf's advice: find a president for the club—a good one, the best one. Don't take the job yourself, he told Rocky—not with everything else on your plate, including having to address the other Wirtz businesses.

Did Reinsdorf have anyone in mind? He didn't, but that was fine. Rocky's mind had already flashed to the perfect candidate.

The Ex-Cub Factor

A few hours before the United Center ceremony to honor Bill Wirtz descended into spectacle, John McDonough, president of the Chicago Cubs, swung his car out of the private parking lot at Wrigley Field, his face hot with his own sense of embarrassment and anguish. Moments earlier, Alfonso Soriano, the team's $136 million leadoff hitter, flared a weak fly ball to right, completing a shocking playoff sweep by the Arizona Diamondbacks and triggering a thunderous chorus of boos to rival the impending debacle later that evening before the Blackhawks home opener.

The Cubs' ugly exit stung as any postseason collapse would—aggravated in this case by the success of the regular season, to say nothing of the continuing misery of the team's century-long World Series drought. For McDonough, the loss felt like a personal failure. A year earlier, after the team had finished with the worst record in the National League, he'd proclaimed that anything less than a World Series ring would be a disappointment. At the end of the 2007 regular season, the team sat atop the Central Division standings, so the first-round sweep at the hands of the Diamondbacks seemed to confirm the cynical view: These were the Cubs. They'd find a way to blow it.

Painful as the outcome was, McDonough's self-flagellation hardly squared with the reality of what he had achieved. After all, the tall, slim, and witty fifty-five-year-old had helped fill Wrigley's seats and create a fervent and obediently forgiving national following. Baseball insiders called him a marketing genius. It was hard to argue, given the Cubs' consistently booming attendance in the face of chronic, almost comical failure.

His modest beginnings only added to his mystique. His humble academic path sprang from humble roots. He grew up on the North Side of Chicago, Cubs territory, but rooted for the lunch-bucket South Side club, the White Sox. In high school, he couldn't make the sports teams and so found himself flipping burgers at McDonald's. Years later, he still recalled the pain of being behind the counter, serving up fries and shakes to classmates from the baseball and basketball teams when they'd pile in exuberantly disheveled from a game.

For college, he wanted to go to one of the elite Catholic schools, but, as he once joked to the *Chicago Tribune*, when Notre Dame and Georgetown heard he was interested, the schools gave him a preemptive rejection. He settled for little St. Mary's University in Winona, Minnesota.

Blessed with an athlete's self-assurance, however, McDonough found his niche among the jocks. He started as an entry-level staffer with the Chicago Sting, the city's professional soccer team during the '70s and '80s, where he discovered a knack for promoting an otherwise unfamiliar product. He got cocky enough that he sought—and won—audiences with two of the city's legendary figures: Papa Bear George Halas and the Baron of the Bottom Line himself, Arthur Wirtz. "I remember going into Arthur's office and seeing this mountain of a man," McDonough says. "I don't intimidate easily, but I think I was shivering. Arthur was not just sports-world royalty, he was Chicago royalty, an honest-to-God tycoon. He asked me about my background and what my aspirations were."

Later, McDonough recalls, he descended the stairs at Chicago Stadium to "a dark cavernous area" for a meeting with Arthur's right-hand man, Bob Pulford. His pitch could not have been more audacious. "I think I was thirty at the time," McDonough says, "and I said, 'I would like to be considered to run the business operation for the Chicago Blackhawks.'" McDonough had brought with him a detailed business plan that included a loaded recommendation: televise home games. "Bob listened for about an hour and was very gracious and very patient," McDonough says. "He told me these are great ideas, but Mr. Wirtz would never go for it."

Not long after—in 1983—McDonough joined the Cubs, and he quickly moved up to the role of chief marketer and spokesman. He frequently had to explain away some idiotic baseball decisions and business moves. But he was also the rare Cubs official who dared to say the team's goal should be to win it all. His talent flowered when the Cubs, year after year, fell woefully short, and he invented ways to raise the ante on non-baseball entertainment. McDonough pioneered unusual fan giveaways—Beanie Babies, most famously—and dreamed up the Cubs Convention, the winter celebration that has subsequently been widely copied among teams.

For years, the announcer Harry Caray pulled his bulk up from his seat during the seventh-inning stretch at home games and, eyes shining behind his signature oversized glasses, belted out a beery version of *Take Me Out to the Ballgame* to a swaying, equally beery crowd. The sing-along became a hallowed Wrigley Field tradition that seemed fated to end when Caray died suddenly in 1998. For fans, the question wasn't inconsequential: should the team drop the ritual, go with a recording, or figure out something new? McDonough's solution was a winner: bring in guest celebrities to sing. And since 1998 fans at Wrigley have been serenaded by everyone from Bill Murray to ex-Cub Ernie Banks to addled British rocker Ozzy Osbourne, whose staggeringly awful, mumble-screech rendition (available on YouTube, though not for the faint of heart) provoked a howl of its own that perhaps the new practice should be reconsidered.

The Cubs enjoyed a few winning years, but for the most part the on-field performance was dismal. But here again, McDonough displayed his brilliance. If the team could not make winning its brand, McDonough helped turn losing into an everyman's virtue. Thus, the team in his era doubled down on "lovable losers," an image cemented into legend when twice the Cubs came close to getting into the World Series, only to fail suddenly and disastrously.

Marketing professionals talk about brands with soul, and that was McDonough's Cubs—not only did the ball club ignite a strong emotional response in consumers, but the team's image invoked a range of positive features from loyalty to modesty to a sense of history. "How can anybody take that ballclub and turn it into 3 million people [in attendance]?" Chicago businessman Lee Stern, an investor in the White Sox, asked about McDonough.

McDonough's appointment in 2006 as Cubs president had raised his portfolio beyond marketing and communications to the on-field performance of the team, and his first year in the larger job had paid off. Entering the 2007 playoffs, McDonough's seemingly foolish World Series boast lay tantalizingly within reach. Even crusty fans allowed themselves to hope when the club's postseason opened against the Diamondbacks. Three games later, McDonough watched in stunned silence as the opposing team's players sprinted across the Wrigley diamond, whooping as they leapt onto an ecstatic pile at the pitcher's mound.

The telephone call came as he wound his way past the dejected throngs that trudged toward side street parking lots. The voice on the other end was Guy Chipparoni, a communications executive and Rocky's new advisor. "I'm calling on behalf of Rocky Wirtz," Chipparoni said. "He would like to meet with you."

Grateful for the distraction, McDonough replied that he'd like to meet Rocky. "And I did want to," McDonough says. "I wanted to express my condolences at the passing of his father." McDonough was leaving town in a couple of days, however, bound for baseball meetings in Orlando. Maybe they could meet in a few weeks?

"And I hung up," says McDonough. "No more than thirty seconds later, the phone rings—it was Chipparoni again. 'I think it's in your best interest to meet before you leave town.'"

"Well, if it's that important," McDonough said. He lived in Elk Grove Village and suggested they meet Saturday at noon at a bar called Champps in Schaumburg. Soon after, McDonough slid into a booth and waited. "I had no idea what he looked like," he says. "Then I see this well-dressed guy come in. He's kind of looking around, so I go over and say 'Rocky? I'm John McDonough.'"

"We talked about family, business philosophies," McDonough recalls. "But I'm still not sure what this is about. I figured he wanted to network, maybe pick my brain about the McCaskeys [owners of the Chicago Bears] or something."

No, Rocky said, leaning in. "I want you to run the Blackhawks. And I have no plan B."

"It was the last thing I thought we were meeting about," McDonough says. "I was amused and flattered at the same time. He was so charismatic and so authentic. So 1:30 turned into 3:30, which turned into 4:30. I called my wife and said, 'We're still here.'

"We had a lot of fun and a lot of laughs," McDonough recalls, "but finally, he said, 'Tell me what you think?' I said, 'I'm really impressed by this, but I'm president of the Cubs. Let me think about it. I'll let you know when I get to Florida if I'm interested.' "

After a bumpy night's sleep, McDonough called some of his friends and asked for their unvarnished opinion. The answer, to a person, was unequivocal: "Every one of them said, 'You're going to leave the Cubs to go run the Blackhawks? John, are you out of your fucking mind?' "

The reactions had the opposite of their intended effect. "The more they said that," says McDonough, "the more inspired I became to do it."

On a Monday, Rocky called McDonough in Florida. "I told him what I thought it would take. He said, 'I'll have an offer to you Wednesday morning at nine o'clock.' "

Sure enough, at nine sharp, "Boom," says McDonough. "I go to the front desk of my hotel and it was coming over in a fax."

Still, McDonough hedged. "I called home and talked to my wife and kids. They were very emotional. 'Are you sure you want to do this? You've invested your life in the Cubs.' "

"Yes," he answered, "I'm sure."

Yet, when he picked up the phone to call Rocky, McDonough hesitated. "I had to remind myself that I'm about to quit the job as president of the Chicago Cubs," he says.

By the time Rocky picked up, however, McDonough was resolute. "I said, 'You've got a deal. Let's go.' "

McDonough made the announcement at a press conference at Wrigley Field and again at a media gaggle at the United Center. But it was only after his first meeting with the Blackhawks' staff that the magnitude of what he faced dawned. "I'm standing there in front of these people and I can see in their eyes that a good percentage of them have checked out—like, 'I don't want to deal with this guy,'" McDonough recalls. "When I realized that most of them were probably going to have to go, I thought, 'This isn't going to be fun.'"

A Change of Channel

One day in October 2007, a few days after Rocky took charge of the team, a curious set of noises—bumps, furniture scrapes, rustling paper, hushed voices—drifted from the northern tip of a bleak row of offices on the nineteenth floor of 680 North Lake Shore Drive. From their hushed warren of cubicles, the few staffers around could see with a discreet glance the source of the muted clamor. The new boss—Rocky—was moving in. His arrival was hardly a surprise. In the wake of Peter's sudden departure, they'd anticipated this moment with a mixture of anxiety and uncertainty. What shocked was the office he had chosen.

For twenty-five years, Arthur's workspace had sat uninhabited and untouched, a frozen-in-time tribute to the late patriarch. From the day of his death, it was understood that the austerely appointed room was off limits. People would no more disturb it than they would hop the velvet rope around Sue the dinosaur at the Field Museum and start swinging on the fossilized bones. Bill had seemed awed by the place, choosing to set up shop at the opposite end of the office row—as if Arthur's ghost might appear and dress him down for presuming he deserved the founder's seat. Rocky considered his father's attitude puzzling, silly even. It was just an office, after all. Besides, Bill was the head of the company—why wouldn't he sit in the chairman's seat? When Rocky suggested as much to Bill, however, he received a gelid stare. "He was not receptive," Rocky recalls.

Bill had insisted that everything remain just as it was when Arthur last sat at his desk. Indeed, on first entering the room as the new chairman, Rocky felt as if he were looking at a museum exhibit. Other than some stacked file boxes stashed inside for lack of more storage space, the place looked just the way Rocky remembered it, from Arthur's pen-and-pencil set to the rotary phone on the immaculate desk to the display cases. The effect was so eerie that Rocky half expected to hear Arthur's voice telling him to take a seat while he made some calls.

Unlike Bill, however, Rocky claimed the office without hesitation. And while he was tickled to display some of Arthur's artifacts—the pen-and-pencil set, for one—he had no qualms about adding his own touches: a comfortable leather couch, some new books to replace the musty tomes in the glass-doored armoire.

Rocky realized that older staff members would be scandalized. Good. They needed a shake-up. Peter, he guessed, would be more appalled than anyone. So be it. Rocky wasn't trying to be provocative. No one had more respect for Arthur than he. When people told him they saw the best parts of the Baron in him—as they often did—he wore the comparison proudly. But that was the point of moving into his grandfather's workspace. What better way to honor the man who created the family business than to engineer its turnaround from behind the same desk? What better way to show he was not afraid of the challenge ahead, but excited to embrace it—to make a break from the past?

Respecting history was fine, but fetishizing it, letting nostalgia overwhelm business sense, stood as one big reason why the Blackhawks were in such a mess. Rocky's father had fretted about his own father's disapproval, even after Arthur was long gone. While admirable to a degree, that fealty accounted in part for Bill's maddening refusal to even *entertain* the notion of airing home games on TV, much less do it. The man who had built the family fortune had decreed the ban and, by God, Bill would uphold the edict if he had to drag the rest of Wirtz Corp. down in the process—and woe unto the man or woman who dared question him on the matter.

It was madness, all of it, Rocky believed, and he was bent on driving the point home in every way he could, starting with rearranging the furniture in a room once considered inviolable. "I wanted everyone in the office to know that we're progressing as a business. That we're moving along. We're not fearful."

Anyway, he had far bigger worries. As the new head of family business, he controlled the entire Wirtz portfolio, including the wholesale liquor business, the real estate holdings, and the banking and insurance divisions. Publicly, he put the best face on the Everest of new responsibilities, assuring the public of the relative health of Wirtz Corp. "If anything, we'll grow our business more," he told the *Tribune* soon after taking over. "We're well-capitalized, we're proud of our balance sheet, and that's a good thing when times are tough."

That last part was true. For all the losses, the company had not fallen into the trap of expanding through borrowing at high interest rates. *Dun & Bradstreet* estimated that the corporation enjoyed roughly $1.3 billion in annual sales and employed some 1,500 staff. The liquor business, under Rocky's hand, had expanded into Nevada, Minnesota, Wisconsin, and Iowa, and the Judge & Dolph distributorship ranked second largest in Illinois. Again, all true, and all to the good.

Behind the scenes, however, cracks spread through the foundation. The liquor industry faced massive consolidation as bigger corporations scrambled to gobble up smaller companies, which meant Rocky had to spend to keep up. Other sectors also battled pressures. The real estate side, which included roughly two thousand apartments, needed attention—"upgrades to all of the systems," Rocky says. The banking side, meanwhile, also found itself struggling. In all, it was an inopportune moment to tap the other family businesses to shore up the precarious financial position of the Hawks, but the size of the emergency—to say nothing of the company's survival—left few alternatives.

The public presumably had some awareness of the team's financial problems—Bill's bombshell interview with the *Toronto Star* a few months before his death saw to that. But no one beyond the most trusted inner circle comprehended the magnitude of the predicament—the year-over-year cash losses in the tens of millions, the inability to make payroll without an infusion from the other Wirtz companies. *Forbes* ranked the Blackhawks—an Original Six team in the third-largest market in the country—sixteenth among thirty NHL franchises, with an estimated value of $179 million. That put Chicago behind such small-market teams as the Tampa Bay Lightning ($199 million) and the Ottawa Senators ($186 million) and far from top-ranked Toronto, whose Maple Leafs were valued at more than $400 million.

Rocky OK'd a series of cash infusions, but he also knew that for the team to survive, it had to stand on its own, just as real estate, liquor, banking, and insurance had to stand on *their* own. As unthinkable as it seems now, in that autumn of 2007, he could not say for certain that the Hawks could pull it off. "For any one of the businesses to be struggling was one thing, but when you had challenges with all of them at the same time, we had major stuff to overcome," he says.

Further imperiling the company was a factor that had already grown from a snowball into a rolling, dangerous, rapidly expanding avalanche. Fourteen months before Bill's death, in July 2006, housing prices in the United States started to slip, then fall. The real estate bubble, as many had predicted, had finally burst, the result of decades of financial deregulation and predatory lending. That crash, in turn, triggered a complex chain of events that would cause the largest stock market free fall since the 1930s—the period when Arthur first began to build the family business—and push the world's financial and monetary systems into chaos, if not to the brink of collapse.

The most catastrophic consequences of the Great Recession, as it is now known, had yet to be felt when Rocky took over, but the first fat drops of the coming storm already spattered much of the economy. The stock market, having peaked at 14,164, had begun its precipitous tumble just after Bill's death. A trickle of mortgage defaults now raged like a run of Amazon rapids. Consumer confidence, already shaky, plummeted.

For a professional sports franchise desperate to lure back fans, the timing could scarcely have been worse, particularly when the team had so deepened the pall. Rocky discovered that in an effort to fill seats Bill had dropped ticket prices to the second-lowest in the league. "We were twenty-eighth or twenty-ninth out of thirty teams," Rocky says. "It was a jump ball between us and Phoenix. When you have the second-lowest ticket price on average and the second-lowest attendance, you've got a real big problem." Bill had reacted in exactly the wrong way—by slashing payroll, including the most crucial department: sales. By doing so, you can save a few bucks, Rocky says, but you can't do what you really need to do: generate new revenue.

Undermining everything was the saddest reality of all, a factor that would have been almost inconceivable a decade earlier: a pervasive and punishing fan apathy. "They weren't the fifth team in a five-team town," says *Daily Herald* columnist Barry Rozner. "They were the 10th team in a five-team town. They didn't exist. They were the worst thing you can possibly be for a sports franchise: They were irrelevant."

Rozner says that growing up he worshipped the Blackhawks. He remembers games at the old Chicago Stadium. "It had toilets that didn't work, the halls smelled like puke, people pissed in the stairwells because the bathrooms were so bad. I mean, the place was a dump," he says, "but, wow, was it a great place to watch a hockey game." The building had excellent sight lines, extraordinary noise, and the one thing no amount of luxury boxes and microbrews can create: mystique. "You'll never find a better place in your life."

After the Stadium came down in 1995 and the Hawks started to play in the new United Center, the team continued to draw until it began its long decline, a plunge "to a depth that no one could have imagined," Rozner says. Suddenly, the United Center version of the Madhouse on Madison bore a different, ignominious appellation: Mausoleum on Madison.

Rocky knew he needed to deliver a bold, sweeping signal of his commitment to shaking things up, and no more potent symbol existed than to start televising home games. Just days after taking over the team, he approached Comcast SportsNet, the local sports network, about the possibility. Officials there were thrilled. They promised to begin clearing space for the following season. No, Rocky said. This season. Silence. "They were aghast," Rocky recalls.

Still, Rocky had leverage, which he did not hesitate to exercise. The team owned a piece of the network, and besides, the positive publicity generated by such an audacious move was incalculable.

After some arm-twisting, the network agreed to air seven games, the first on November 11, less than two months after Bill's death. Rocky would have preferred more games, but he recognized that what counted was the symbolism of the move. No other gesture would more clearly demonstrate his willingness to break from the past and his father.

The big problem now, however, was selling spots to advertisers, an effort that went so comically wrong that even Rocky has to laugh today. Rocky himself played salesman, inviting executives from some of the world's top beverage sellers to dinner to make his pitch. In one such meeting, at Gibson's Bar & Steakhouse, Rocky tried to create a sense of urgency by using a tactic any car salesman or real estate agent might recognize: warning the client that he needed to act fast to beat out some other very interested customers. "I fibbed and said all the [advertising] packages under $100,000 are taken. The phones are ringing off the hook. It sat there like a turd on the table."

Things got even worse. "I couldn't even sell personal injury guys," Rocky says. The ratings didn't help. "I think we went from a .4 share with the first game to a .6 with the second." With each ratings point representing roughly thirty-five thousand viewers, "it was less than the Home Shopping Network had."

In terms of publicity, however, the move had exactly the effect Rocky had hoped for: it was a smash hit. "You read correctly," *Sun-Times* columnist Jay Mariotti wrote. "TV cameras with little red lights, the very technology that drives the multibillion-dollar sports machine as we know it, actually will be in the building when the Hawks are playing. What's next around here? Clean and honest politicians? Accurate weather forecasters? Yogurt replacing Italian beef and deep-dish pizza? It's astounding. [Bill] Wirtz's kid needed all of 26 days to buck his father's cardinal rule and announce a radical philosophical shift. Yo, Rocky? Where have you been all our lives?"

"People in the building are in shock," Rozner wrote. "The days of 'imperial bureaucracy' are over. Decisions that used to take weeks to filter all the way through the office to Bill Wirtz are now taking minutes."

"Sure Dad isn't going to turn over in his grave?" Mariotti asked.

In a lively press conference discussing the new policy, Rocky was asked whether televising games had ever been discussed with his father. "Absolutely," he told reporters, treating them to a glimpse of his dry sense of humor. "And the talk stopped about there. We'd have a meeting in a boardroom, and he'd say, 'All those in favor signify by saying aye. All opposed, resign.'" Still, he argued that Bill would have loved the move. "I think he'd be the first one . . . to pat me on the back," Rocky said. Today, Rocky concedes the statement was a bit of a stretch. "Would he be happy? I think he would have been happy with the result. He just wouldn't agree with anything we did to get there."

In any case, Rocky harbored no doubts about the call. "There was never, ever a second thought," he says. "I did what I thought was right for the company. Whatever that is. You know, if that was the same as Dad, then great. If it was different, that's OK too."

But Rocky's ambitions reached far higher than simply pulling the team back from the edge of disaster. "One of the goals I talked to [John McDonough] about that first day was to walk down any street in the world and see some Blackhawk paraphernalia. I wanted the team to be a gold standard organization in the way that the Yankees are in baseball." On a more personal level, Rocky says, "I wanted to get the Wirtz name to where people didn't cringe at it."

At the time, the task loomed almost absurdly tall. "There were whole generations of Hawks fans who said I will never go to another game as long as a Wirtz is in charge," Rozner says.

McDonough recognized the problem—he saw a level of antipathy that reached heights he'd never encountered in his career as a sports executive. He warned Rocky that "the changes are going to come fast and they're not going to be for the faint of heart," starting with a staff housecleaning. Rocky had already taken the first steps. Even before McDonough came on, Rocky had moved senior Hawks vice president Bob Pulford, a favorite of Bill's and formerly an untouchable within the organization, away from the team and into a role with Wirtz Corp.

That, McDonough knew, would only be the beginning. There needed to be a reckoning. "I told Rocky that I wanted an organization with a lot of high-octane—a young, dynamic, enthusiastic group of people that wanted to be part of something that had never been done before," recalls McDonough. "A lot of these decisions are going to come off as cold-blooded. They're not meant to be. They will be because I have an obligation to you and your family and to the fans to try and build the best organization in our industry."

More bluntly put, "This is the heavyweight division," he told his new boss. "Our names are on this now. My name's on it, your name is on it.

"I remember exactly what he said," McDonough recalls, "and this is why he is a great owner and someone who is a mentor, and someone I admire so deeply: he said, 'John, do what you need to do.' He said the same when we met later. 'Nobody is sacred. You have the ability to make the decisions. Please keep me involved, but you have autonomy.' "

McDonough advised that the hockey side could no longer take precedence over the business side. In the past, the team's front office had been paid more and generally been treated with far more respect than the business side of the franchise. In fact, the brass close to the players often looked down their noses at the people running the business. If the turnaround was going to succeed, McDonough said—and Rocky agreed—they had to be on equal footing. "Rocky and I basically said those words at the same time," he recalls. "Just because the hockey guys have their names in the paper doesn't mean they're above the business side in the hierarchy. The business guys are bringing in tens of millions of dollars—hundreds of millions. There has to be mutual respect."

On a brighter note, the team's prospects that season weren't entirely bleak. By his own admission, general manager Dale Tallon had enjoyed only hit-or-miss success with the players he'd brought in since being named to the post two years earlier. But a year before Rocky took over, Tallon connected on a home run. With the third pick in the 2006 draft, the Hawks took Jonathan Toews, the gifted center who in short order would become the cornerstone of the franchise. The next year, with the first selection, Tallon drafted Patrick Kane, another superstar in the making. Coach Denis Savard had struggled for success, but he'd also made the most of the talent he'd been given. With this new infusion, things could only get better.

Meanwhile, another area needed immediate shoring up: media relations. Bill had pummeled the press for so long that sports reporters treated the team with disdain. What's more, because the Hawks had been so bad for so long, many of the newspapers had stopped sending reporters to cover away games.

Rocky's solution was a charm offensive. He turned to Chipparoni, who thought the idea a good one. "I had said to him in passing that the only way you're going to get out of this maze is to treat this like a political campaign," Chipparoni says. "Not because you're trying to win over people, but because you've got to clear the air on all this."

The campaign would aim at restoring the brand, and the only person who could lead it was the new owner. "I said, 'You've gotta fight for every inch,'" Chipparoni recalls. "'You need to send the message to the marketplace that the status quo isn't going to be acceptable.'"

Rocky made the rounds in person, visiting with beat reporters, columnists, editors, and executives at the *Sun-Times*, *Tribune*, *Crain's Chicago Business*, and the *Daily Herald*. After years of being ripped by Bill, some media folks received the visitor with wariness. "When he came in, some of them were peering over the tops of their cubicles like, 'Uh, oh,'" recalls Chipparoni. "But he came hat in hand and basically said, 'Look, I understand we've not been relevant. I understand that you've not been treated well. Just give us a chance.'"

In Rozner's case, Rocky sat with him for several hours at a restaurant. "I don't think I knew what to expect," Rozner recalls. "I'm sure I made reference to being surprised that anyone in his family would even speak to me. I had written some hard truths about the team for a long time. But he made it clear he had no problem with me, that we had a clean slate."

To Rozner's surprise, what Rocky really seemed to want was information. "He started asking me questions. So I started telling him everything, and I mean everything. And it was ugly. I told him a lot of ugly truths.

"I told him everything I thought about the organization, the level of incompetency. There was no front office to speak of, they basically had no sales department, no marketing department, no advertising, nothing. If there were ten people working in the front office outside of ticket sales, I would have been surprised. I gave Rocky chapter and verse on everyone working there and the roles they were in, and who was in the wrong roles."

Rozner's analysis was so unrelentingly negative that at one point, he recalls, Chipparoni interrupted: "Lighten up a little would you? You're going awfully strong here."

"I looked at Rocky and said, 'Do you want me to lighten up?' And he said, 'I'm fine.' So I continued. We went for about three hours with Rocky just listening and asking questions. I don't know how seriously he took anything that I had to say or how useful it was, but he definitely listened closely."

Realizing the importance of reaching suburban fans, Rocky invited *Daily Herald* publisher Doug Ray and his wife to dinner and a Blackhawks game at the United Center. "That was unheard of," Ray says. Bill had only ever invited Ray to the office for a tongue-lashing. In contrast, Rocky "was a great host. I think it was his way of saying, 'We care about you, we care about the suburbs.' He made a real effort to connect with us and we haven't forgotten that. We cover the Blackhawks honestly and fairly, but I think it's fair to say he has become a good friend of the paper."

The reviews of Rocky's performance in those first weeks were almost universally positive, from fans and the media. *Almost.* A few observers questioned whether Rocky was moving *too* fast. "From a fan's perspective it's great—he's doing everything right," Weinberg, the Chicago attorney, told *Chicago* magazine. "On a deeper psychological level, I think one has to ask, 'What's going on here?' With the things Rocky has done, and the speed with which he's done them, there's almost an 'In your face, Dad' quality. The guy wasn't even cold in the ground before they decided they were going to make all these decisions and undo everything the old man stood for."

The speed and scope of the changes also raised the eyebrows of columnist Bob Verdi. "As soon as Bill died and Rocky took over and started making these changes, I thought, 'Wow, I wonder what the old man would think about this,'" Verdi told *Chicago*. "I wondered, is this respectful—not only to do it, but to do it so soon?" On the other hand, Verdi acknowledged that Rocky had little choice. "The franchise was in such a state of disrepair, what greater service could

Rocky perform for the family name than to roll up his sleeves and fix what he thought needed fixing?"

Some worried that McDonough was going to usher in the "Cubification" of the Hawks—a marketing plan filled with gimmicks and razzle-dazzle that would rob the team of its gritty appeal and fill the stands with people who cared less about hockey than about the spectacle.

Secondhand, Rocky also heard grumblings from some members of his family about the breathtakingly quick dismantling of their father's most sacrosanct philosophies. Far from joining the vast throngs asking what took him so long, the family wondered how he could be so callous, so disloyal, so . . . cold-blooded? What possible reason could he have for changing so much so fast?

Resurrection

As the last heady months of autumn 2007 chilled into the gray prospect of approaching winter, lovers of the city's hockey team discovered a multiplying mound of wondrous gifts piling up under their Christmas trees. Each day, it seemed, brought fresh delights as Rocky, playing Santa, granted wish after wish. The new owner seemed bent on dismantling the wall his father had built between fans and their beloved Blackhawks, between the Blackhawks and the hope of a new day.

There was the jaw-dropping news of games on TV, the charm offensive with the papers, Bob Pulford being moved out of the United Center and into 680 North Lake Shore. Rocky's McDonough coup elicited gleeful puns such as "Cold Steal on Ice" (the *Tribune*) and "Presidential Steal" (the *Sun-Times*). The announcement that Rocky planned to open talks with John McDonough and Pat Foley, the beloved play-by-play man unceremoniously dumped in 2006 by Bill Wirtz over a contract dispute, brought widespread cheer.

"To think of where the organization was two months ago—still stuck in the '50s—and to see it now is one of the most extraordinary turnarounds of upper management in Chicago sports history," Rozner wrote on November 21. "Suddenly, because of Rocky Wirtz, it's okay to admit you're a Blackhawks' fan again."

Wayne Gretzky, perhaps the greatest player and ambassador in NHL history, expressed his delight at the club's budding turnaround.

"They've gone through some tough times," Gretzky, then coach of the Phoenix Coyotes, said before a game against the Hawks in late November. "It's great to see. This is one of the great franchises and great sports cities in America." Gretzky called Patrick Kane the "best player in the draft," and heaped praise on Jonathan Toews. "When you get an eighteen-year-old like Kane and a nineteen-year-old like Toews . . . it goes a long way for a franchise and an organization."

Letters to the editor bubbled with praise from fans who a few short months earlier penned nothing but venom: "Positive stories in the paper! Stories of rehab, confrontations. Apathy replaced by competitive spirit, enthusiasm, hope, and even a few victories," Ed Gabler of Glendale Heights wrote to the *Daily Herald*. "Although we've been led along this path in the past, I truly believe we have turned a corner."

The team itself seemed turbocharged by the daily infusion of octane, though not always for the better. As the 2007–2008 season unfolded, the Hawks, like a novice driving a hot new sports car, lurched wildly between thrilling wins and bumpy detours, giving fans "more thrills, chills, and spills than a rush-hour snowstorm on the Kennedy," as one reporter wrote.

In January, at the midpoint of the season, the team's record stood at exactly .500—nineteen wins, nineteen losses, and three ties, six points out of the final playoff spot and struggling after the fifth loss in what would be a seven-game losing streak. With twenty-four goals and forty-seven assists between them, Kane and Toews drew praise. Patrick Sharp, meanwhile, rode the crest of a career year with twenty goals and thirteen assists. But the play of netminder Nikolai Khabibulin whipsawed between dazzling and dreadful, and a raft of injuries on the team's front line—in one stretch they had eight players go down in a single week—further doomed any chance at consistency.

Just as fans grew antsy, however, McDonough reached into his Santa bag and produced another shiny package: the return from exile of the Big Three legends of Blackhawks lore—Stan Mikita, Tony Esposito, and Bobby Hull.

As with so many of the moves that were made, reconnecting with the aggrieved former players seemed both obvious and easy. Why not call up the old superstars? Fans would love it. Surely the players would jump at the chance to heal old wounds. But it took a diplomatic miracle to turn fantasy into reality, particularly when it came to Bobby Hull. "Rocky and I had a conversation about the importance of bringing these guys back," McDonough recalls, "but I didn't know how bad Bobby's relationship was with Bill or with [Bob] Pulford."

The new Hawks president quickly learned. Far from healing all wounds, time had inflamed them. There wasn't bad blood; there was boiling blood. When McDonough dialed up Hull, "It was as if he'd been waiting thirty-six years for that call," McDonough says. "He really let me have it."

Here's how McDonough recalls Hull's response: "They screwed me in '71 and I've never felt welcome there for all I've done. I propped that franchise up and I was the biggest star they had and they crapped all over me? Screw you."

Hull didn't stop there. His tirade continued and McDonough just listened. "It kept getting worse and worse," the Hawks exec says. "I let him empty the bag." At one point, Hull paused long enough to ask if McDonough was still on the line. When McDonough answered yes, Hull opened back up with both barrels. Finally, the old winger had spent all his bullets, and McDonough got right to the point. "Bobby," he said, "I understand. Is there a chance you could come in and meet Rocky?"

Hull growled no, that it would just be "The same old shit." Moments later, however, the player softened. "Let me think about it," he said.

With instructions to call back in a week, McDonough let it lie. Rocky, meanwhile, stepped in with a phone call. Hull agreed to meet on one condition: that Rocky himself attend. "He knew me from when I was a kid and he'd been following the changes we were making," Rocky says.

As the conversation continued, McDonough made his pitch. "This is a different ownership group, a different organization," he told Hull. "We think you're a major part of this organization, and we're going to treat you with dignity and respect. We want you to be around as often as you can. It's going to be a great experience for you, for the organization, for the fans." Hull, of course, would be compensated. If he were interested, McDonough would work up a contract.

Hull said he needed another week. When McDonough called with an offer, Hull again balked. "No way."

McDonough relayed the response to Rocky. "Do what you need to do," Rocky answered.

When the Hawks president tried again, Hull at last relented. (McDonough declined to divulge the terms.) "I get chills thinking about it right now," says McDonough. "It was a watershed moment in the history of this franchise. Nobody in their wildest dreams believed Bobby Hull, 'the Golden Jet,' would return."

Among the shocked were Mikita and Esposito, also being pursued by McDonough. "Like Bobby, I had given up," Mikita told the *Tribune*. "Then the phone rings." Hull was in, McDonough said. Mikita and Esposito had the same response: "If Bobby's back, we're back," McDonough recalls.

The festivities to honor Hull and Mikita took place at the United Center on a Saturday night before a packed house of rowdy fans, less than six months after the disastrous ceremony honoring Bill Wirtz. (Esposito would be given his own night a few weeks later.) This time, however, thunderous applause rang through the stadium. A black-and-white highlight reel showed Mikita darting through lines to beat a flailing goalie up top and Hull unleashing his blistering slap shot. Current players skated onto the ice wearing either a number 9 or a number 21 sweater, the respective numbers of Hull and Mikita. In the wings, perched out of sight on a '57 Chevy convertible—the year chosen in honor of Hull's first season—the two former stars watched with broad smiles, Hull at one point wiping his eyes.

The crowd erupted when Rocky, looking slightly sheepish, stepped forth in a dark blue suit and tie. Making his way onto a strip of red carpet that had been laid on the ice, he stepped to a lectern decorated with 9s and 21s. "Bobby and Stan, your honor, commitment, and leadership over the years defined Chicago Blackhawk hockey on the ice," Rocky said. "You guys are larger than life because you played larger than life. Generations of fans, past, present, and future, will always remember you."

Rocky went on to thank the fans with a not-so-subtle message as a punch line: "Wherever you are, in person, listening on the radio, or watching on TV at home . . ." At the mention of television, the stadium exploded, and Rocky, beaming, had to wait several seconds for the noise to die down. "Thank you for listening, thank you for watching, and, most importantly, thank you for coming back."

When the vintage Chevy carrying Hull and Mikita appeared, the crowd erupted in an ear-splitting reception. In his very brief remarks, Hull, silver-haired, square-jawed, his round face bearing the mashed-in, lunch-bucket mug of a skyscraper welder, graciously avoided any mention of the animus that had marked the decades leading to this moment. Instead, he talked about his boyhood dream, his years in Chicago, and his delight at being back. "In nineteen and fifty seven, I made a boyhood dream come true to play in the National Hockey League," Hull said. "Little did I know that for the next fifteen years I would be living in the greatest city in the world and playing in front of the greatest hockey fans in all the world."

Mikita, who played all of his twenty-one seasons with the Blackhawks, followed. "I spent so many years proudly wearing the Indian head sweater," he said. "But tonight I'm even more proud to be welcomed back and be a part of the great moments that lie ahead for this great franchise." The last line may have brought the biggest roar of all.

The only thing missing from that perfect night was a win. With less than a month left in the season, the Hawks were fighting for the playoffs. They'd won their past three games, but desperately needed another victory. The San Jose Sharks, however, eked out a 3–2 thriller. The loss dropped the Hawks to six points out of the eighth and final playoff spot with fourteen games left in the season.

The Hawks' win-a-couple, lose-a-couple rollercoaster continued for the rest of the season, including three straight losses after the ceremony night. They kept hopes alive into the final four days. On April 3, however, for the second night in a row, the Nashville Predators—the team just ahead of them—came back to beat the St. Louis Blues, extending the Hawks playoff drought to six years.

The Blackhawks' next game came against Vancouver, and something extraordinary happened. In the final home game of the season, the team played with passion in one of its best performances, beating their new nemesis 3–1. The win was the Hawks' fourth in a row, played before the biggest crowd of the season, 21,919. On the way back to the locker room, one of the players made a spur-of-the-moment suggestion: "Let's go back out." The team did, tossing gloves and sticks into the stands and waving their gratitude to the crowd, which rewarded the players with a standing ovation.

In the days that followed, the fan base seemed more optimistic than ever. The team may have missed the playoffs, but it had enjoyed its best season in six years. Toews and Kane were no longer promising rookies, they were future all-stars, cornerstones, and perhaps Hall of Famers.

The financial resurgence in seven short months was astonishing. Ticket sales had shot up 45 percent, with attendance going from an average of seven thousand to eight thousand at the beginning of the season to twenty thousand at the end. The team sold out twelve times and leapt from twenty-ninth in the league in attendance to nineteenth. Merchandise sales at the Hawk Quarters store on Michigan Avenue—since rechristened the Blackhawks Store per McDonough's order—had risen 151 percent; sales were up more than 180 percent at the Fandemonium store in the United Center. When McDonough announced the first annual fan convention for the upcoming July—an innovation he had brought to the Cubs—the event sold 350 hotel rooms overnight.

The team still lost money, but nowhere near the staggering $31 million of the previous year. The resurgence was all the more stunning given the collapsing economy. Rocky's philosophy to "sell our way out" of the cash crisis had paid off—and the push was only beginning.

Just after the end of the season, McDonough hired an ad agency to rebrand the team, an effort that would start by discarding the current, rather puzzling slogan, "Red Rising." The team also announced a joint marketing initiative with the White Sox. Meanwhile, the housecleaning McDonough had promised began in earnest. Shortly after the end of the season, Jim DeMaria, the Blackhawks longtime PR man, left, making him the third marketing and media person to exit since McDonough took over as club president.

McDonough had other plans afoot. In mid-July, after he all but literally browbeat NHL commissioner Gary Bettman, the team announced that the NHL had chosen the Hawks to host the second annual Winter Classic, a New Year's Day game played outdoors. The format had proved wildly successful earlier that year when on a snowy Tuesday in Buffalo, in the home stadium of the NFL's Buffalo Bills, the Pittsburgh Penguins beat the Buffalo Sabres 2–1 before a crowd of 71,217—more than three times the size of a United Center sellout.

In Chicago, the venue would be McDonough's old stomping grounds—Wrigley Field—and the opponent would be the Detroit Red Wings, the Blackhawks' biggest rival. "We knew the timing was right," says Bettman. "If we had tried that in 2004, nobody would have shown up."

Just days later, some ten thousand fans attended the three-day Blackhawks Convention at the Hilton Chicago. McDonough opened the event by announcing that twenty-year-old Jonathan Toews would be the team captain—the first captain since Martin Lapointe in 2006. He also announced that Keith Magnuson's number 3 uniform would be retired prior to the upcoming season. Meanwhile, Frank Pellico, whose organ music was largely quieted after Rocky took over, would no longer have a diminished role.

As expected, the fans roared their approval as the players, waving from a ballroom balcony, were called out one by one. No one, however, was prepared for the reaction when Rocky was introduced. Chants of "Rock-y! Rock-y!" thundered through the ballroom. Cameras flashed as if he were a leading man emerging from a limo on a Hollywood red carpet. "It was surreal," Rocky admits.

"People just don't react to owners that way," says McDonough.

Not everyone, however, was gushing. Rocky's brothers and sisters, led by Peter and Gail, were unimpressed if what Rocky was hearing was true, giving him little credit for the team's turnaround. Tallon had drafted Toews and Kane. The pieces were already in place, went the reasoning. Anyone could have done it.

A Tough Call

The praise heaped on Rocky through the summer of 2008 continued apace into the coming autumn, as the Blackhawks found themselves the most talked about team in hockey, if not all of sport.

It had been an eventful few months. For one glorious weekend in July, the Blackhawks convention transformed the Chicago Hilton into the Madhouse on Michigan, whipping fans into a red, white, and black frenzy that spilled out of the hotel into neighboring bars and down the side streets. Rocky could barely find a moment for himself without someone offering a beery thank you. On the convention's second day, for example, he stole into the coolness of the Hilton bar, Kitty O'Sheas, in search of a quiet drink, but "people kept coming up to me, wanting to buy me a drink. You obviously want to be humble and gracious—it's not about you, after all. The crazy thing is that we hadn't done anything yet."

Actually, the Hawks had improved the season before to the point that—but for a break here and there—the team might have sneaked into the playoffs. A new marketing push was underway, complete with a new slogan—"One Goal"—that replaced the ill-advised "Red Rising." The resurgence on ice and off triggered a stampede for season tickets so large that even a beefed up sales staff struggled to keep up with the demand.

The numbers surpassed anything even Rocky could have imagined. In less than a year, the team had more than tripled season ticket sales—from an embarrassing second-worst-in-the-league 3,400 when Bill died to a franchise-record 13,500. If not for a team-mandated cap on season tickets, the Hawks might have sold out every seat in the arena in advance.

The sales helped replenish the coffers of a team that a year before could not make payroll a week into the season, but whatever gains that were made were necessarily plowed back into the organization. By now, for example, McDonough had tripled the front office staff to seventy-five, including his right-hand man, Jay Blunk, brought over from the Cubs. The team also upgraded its facilities, building a private locker room, workout area, and offices at the Hawks practice facility, Johnny's IceHouse West. Rocky also pushed the team payroll to the league maximum limit of $56.8 million.

Meanwhile, the full effects of the declining Dow were only beginning to be felt. Soon the economy would shed 700,000 to 800,000 jobs a month, triggering crisis after crisis in markets in the United States and around the world. As a precaution, NFL commissioner Roger Goodell issued a memo to teams, warning that they should seek to control costs and explore additional revenue streams beyond ticket sales. Professional baseball teams offered promotions such as gas cards and buy-now, pay-later season tickets.

The intensity of the enthusiasm around the Blackhawks, however, allowed the team to actually *raise* ticket prices slightly.

The Hawks success proved a boon for the Wirtz Corp. as a whole. In a reversal of the previous year, the franchise that was once taking on water at an alarming rate was still losing money, but had stabilized.

The real estate portfolio needed building improvements, for example. But when Rocky asked how much was in the capital improvements budget, he was met with blank looks. "There was no budget," he says.

The Wirtz banking interests were facing other challenges. Things looked slightly brighter on the liquor side. By the fall of 2008, Rocky had closed a deal to acquire another distributor—critical in the swiftly accelerating trend toward consolidation. But that also meant a massive cash outlay.

"We were plugging holes in a dyke," Rocky says. With Wirtz Corp. itself tottering, "we had to do all of it." Had the Blackhawks continued hemorrhaging tens of millions a year, "the whole company could have been pulled under."

One possible escape hatch—to sell the team—wasn't really a possibility. For one, the emotional and financial implications of such a move were too harsh to contemplate. The Blackhawks had been in the Wirtz family for more than a half century, the crown jewel of all that Arthur had built. To sell would be to rip the heart out of the company and stain Rocky's legacy. Besides, the team's value at the time—estimated to be about $179 million—was disgracefully low. What's more, selling the team would most likely mean surrendering the company's half stake in the United Center, another crippling blow. In any case, under the terms of Arthur's succession plan, Rocky would need the approval of all the Wirtz siblings to sell a major asset—a vote he would be unlikely to get.

As it was, the Hawks financial surge made the point moot. So robust was the growth of the business, in fact, that Rocky was able to put dollars where they mattered most: with the team itself. The investment was crucial. The splashy off-ice moves had generated excitement, but they'd also represented a promise: that Rocky cared as much about winning as about marketing schemes. He had ignited expectations.

In their 2008–2009 season previews, sports writers from *USA Today* to *Sports Illustrated* to *Hockey News* tapped the team to end its six-year playoff drought and possibly push deep into the playoffs. Rocky himself had raised the stakes by announcing that his goal was to win a Stanley Cup. Rocky recognized the risks of his candor. Few things would be crueler to fans who had suffered through the Hawks' recent past than to raise hopes, only to dash them by neglecting the team's weaknesses.

To that end, the team's top executives—McDonough, Tallon, and assistant general manager Stan Bowman—landed the hottest free agent on the market, Buffalo Sabres defenseman Brian Campbell. They also signed Cristobal Huet, the stellar goalie for the Washington Capitals. Rocky knew the lavish contracts they were given would raise eyebrows. Campbell was the NHL's top all-star vote getter among Eastern Conference defensemen and would add much needed strength on that end of the ice. But many hockey followers considered the eight-year, $57.12 million deal—the largest contract in team history—far beyond Campbell's value.

Huet was a hot goalie, but $22.4 million over four years seemed almost foolhardy, given that the club owed another goalie, Nikolai Khabibulin, millions on his own megadeal. Tallon put the best face on the huge outlays. "We decided we'd try to make an impact today to give our fans something to get excited about," he told reporters. The reality, as Rocky knew all too well, was that Chicago had been backed into a corner when it came to landing top free agents. Bill's penny-pinching and stubborn haggling had chased away half a dozen stars at least. If the team were to have any chance, Hawks management had to prove the franchise was serious.

Training camp opened on September 19 with the kind of fan-friendly extravaganza that was quickly becoming the hallmark of the Wirtz-McDonough era and all but overshadowed the actual practice. For a fee, fans could attend the first-ever "Training Camp Festival," a daylong series of events that included a 5K run/walk/skate, a three-on-three hockey tournament, live music, and interactive games.

Over the next three weeks, the Hawks got down to business—but almost from the start, McDonough, Tallon, and others perceived a troubling lack of energy. As high as expectations were, the practices seemed flat and uninspired.

So were the first two games of the season. The puzzlingly lackluster play that characterized training camp repeated in a 4–2 loss to the New York Rangers before a sellout crowd at Madison Square Garden. The team was outskated, outgunned, and outhustled. They turned the puck over too many times. Huet, making his debut, contributed almost directly to the Rangers' first goal by leaving a rebound in front of the net. Campbell provided a bright spot when he banked a pass off the base of the Rangers' goal to Patrick Kane, who sizzled a one-timer past goalie Henrik Lundqvist. But another broken play in the third period led to a Rangers goal that put the game out of reach. The team played better in its second game against the Washington Capitals, jumping out to a 2–0 lead, but the Hawks allowed Caps superstar Alex Ovechkin to score twice and the team fell in another 4–2 defeat.

Barely into the season, columnists grew restless, especially after the grand entrance the team made for its home opener. Dressed in suits, the players emerged from black limos and walked a red carpet into the United Center. "It looks like Academy Awards night in Hollywood here in the old gray West Side neighborhood," jibed the *Tribune's* Mike Downey. "You wonder if Joan Rivers will show up to ask who designed that chic Native American shirt." Before the game, there was yet another ceremony, with Rocky again making promises of success. And once again, the Hawks lost, this time 3–2 in a shootout. With the team now 0–3, *Sun-Times* columnist Greg Couch had seen enough hoopla. "Let me just say this," he wrote the next day. "No more ceremonies. The next one comes on the night they clinch a playoff spot."

Those media grumblings were just the beginning of a suddenly cooler tone toward the "new" Hawks—and Rocky. The mood was to be expected given the slow start. Less anticipated was a darkly personal attack leveled against Rocky by Mark Weinberg, the Chicago attorney who had spent years savaging both the team and Bill in the *Blue Line*. Weinberg and his partner Steve Kohn had eventually dropped the venture, citing slim profits, but prior to the 2008–9 season, Weinberg decided to put out a special edition. In it, he suggested that the speed and scope of Rocky's overhaul grew out of his desire to settle scores with his father. Even more loaded was a second accusation: Rocky had forced Peter out to quench a "desperate" longing to be in the spotlight.

That issue of the *Blue Line* came with a comic supplement, dedicated to lampooning "St. Rocky." The cover featured a photo with Rocky's head superimposed over a robed torso clearly meant to be Jesus Christ. The text opened with a mock Gospel ridiculing the months of positive coverage Rocky had received after Bill's death: "Into a city desperately seeking a Savior to bring a once-proud hockey franchise that had died back to life, there came a man, no ordinary mortal, who promised to resurrect the team and its fan base and lead them to the promised land."

When I met Weinberg at his North Side home years later, he acknowledged that he did not know the story behind the fraught relationship of Rocky, his father, and brother, nor did he realize the dire financial straits the team had been in. Still, he defended his criticisms, explaining that he had "done a complete 180" about Bill. "I realized that the man had a certain integrity about things," such as not putting games on TV. Weinberg admitted he may have gone a little overboard criticizing Rocky, but he stood by his basic premise: that the changes Rocky made were born of an unnamed vendetta. "Obviously, once Bill died, Rocky was free to do anything he wants, but to me, he dissed his dad." In the *Blue Line*, Weinberg was more direct. Rocky's actions, he wrote, "have been marked by a bizarre and determined effort to diminish his father's legacy." As evidence, he cited a single quote, misattributed to Rocky (John McDonough made the comment), which likened the Blackhawks to an "80-year-old expansion team."

Given his history, Weinberg's accusations showed a bizarre deference to the Wirtz family history with the Blackhawks. By then, Rocky says that word had drifted to him through the grapevine that his siblings—none of whom agreed to talk to me for this book—were resentful of what they saw as a form of betrayal and remained dismissive of the team's success. Rocky says that his brother and sisters apparently thought that the team had been set up to succeed before he took over—that the Hawks would have done just fine without him.

On a different front, in September 2010, the siblings filed a lawsuit against Rocky over their shares in a lucrative Las Vegas and Minneapolis–St. Paul Coors distributorship of which Rocky owned 51 percent, claiming he was withholding information and devaluing their stakes in handling Bill's affairs. The suit would eventually be settled, but the fact that it was even filed revealed the ugliness of the rift within the family.

Peter's behavior that year followed the pattern. The season before, after his abrupt resignation, he still attended Blackhawks games. "We had a suite he could use," Rocky says. "He would kind of come in through the back door with a key and sit in there and never come out." Starting in 2008, however, he stopped coming altogether. In May 2009, he sold his Bismarck concessions business to a firm called Levy Enterprises, completely severing any ties to the family business.

The people who know Rocky best, from business associates to business rivals, refute the suggestion that ax grinding or personal payback drove Rocky's makeover of the team. They outright scoff at the notion that Rocky was indulging a secret desire for fame. "Rocky couldn't care less about attention," says Charles Merinoff, Rocky's business partner in the liquor outfit, Breakthru Beverage Group. "He has no ego. It's the most bizarre thing I've ever seen in a businessman." More to the point, neither Rocky nor anyone else could have guessed the rock-star-level attention his tenure would trigger.

As for motives, "in every difficult situation that I've had with Rocky, his intentions have always been good—always asking what is best for the company. We don't always agree, sometimes we very much disagree, but I have never, ever—not for one second—questioned his motives. It's always what's best for the business, what's best for the shareholders."

• • •

On October 15, the Blackhawks managed their first win of the season, a 4–1 victory over the Phoenix Coyotes. Even so, the Hawks stunned Chicago and the hockey world by abruptly firing head coach Denis Savard. Rocky knew the sacking would be the first real test of faith in the new era. "He was a Hall of Famer," Rocky says. "Every time you walked in the building you saw his number 18 jersey hanging in the rafters."

Still, as early as preseason, it became clear to Tallon and McDonough that Savard was struggling and needed to be replaced. "He was coaching against guys with far more experience," Rocky says. "He had 150 games against coaches with 500, 600 games under their belts. It just wasn't fair. You can feel horrible and sad, but you can't let that affect sound business decisions."

The hard decision grew from a number of factors. While well intentioned and certainly passionate about the team, Savard had struggled with technical aspects of coaching, such as line matchups and strategy.

Before breaking the news to Savard, however, the team needed a replacement. "So we said, 'Who's out there?'" Rocky recalls. Tallon found their answer in the team's newly hired pro scout, who also happened to be the former head coach with the Colorado Avalanche.

Joel Quenneville is a good man, Tallon said in meetings with Rocky and McDonough. "He's been a head coach, an assistant coach, he won the Stanley Cup as assistant coach in Colorado." In the top job at St. Louis, he led the Blues to seven straight playoff berths. He left for the head coaching job at Colorado in 2004, only to see the season canceled by a strike. The next year he led the Avalanche to a first-round upset of the Dallas Stars. Two years later, in 2007, he earned his 400th victory.

Quenneville came with risks, however. When Colorado didn't meet his contract demands, he told the GM to kiss off, Rocky says. And just a few weeks before, Quenneville had been arrested for driving under the influence. "That was out there and it was a mistake," Rocky says. "But he had taken complete responsibility for it. He admitted, 'I shouldn't have been behind the wheel,' and said it would not happen again. That's when we realized that we had to pull the trigger. So Dale said, 'Let's get him on the phone. I'll talk to Denis.'"

The team struck the deal with Quenneville and Tallon informed Savard. Afterwards, Rocky called Savard. "I said to him, 'Denis, it's unfortunate. We put you in a position that wasn't fair. Our job is to set you up not to fail and you were set up to fail.'" Rocky added that they still wanted him as part of the organization.

"He was really good," Rocky recalls. "He said, 'Well, I'm going to go to Mexico. Let me think about it.'"

While Savard mulled the offer (he would eventually accept), Tallon broke the news—first to the players, then to the public. Both reacted with shock and, in the case of the media, some fairly harsh criticism. "I'll admit I shed a few tears last night just thinking about it," Patrick Kane said after practice the next day. "This is not very fun. He took the fall for us. I was pretty close with Savvy. It's tough to see these things happen. You'd be sad if it happened to anyone, but especially your first coach—the one you pretty much grew with last year."

"A One-Way Commitment," blared the banner headline in the next day's *Sun-Times* sports section. "In end, Savard cared more about Hawks than they did about him." Like Weinberg's potshots, that, too, was unfair. The truth, Rocky says, was that Bill Wirtz had hired Savard for two reasons having nothing to do with coaching ability: because he was a fan favorite and because he was willing to coach for the modest salary Bill was offering. "Dad hated to pay coaches," Rocky says. "So there was no way to get the top names."

As for the critics, there was only one way to prove them wrong: start winning.

The Hawks did.

On December 28, in fact, with a 4–1 victory over the Minnesota Wild, they accomplished what no other Blackhawks team had managed in the 82 previous seasons: they won their ninth game in a row. In the twenty-nine games since Savard's firing, the Hawks had lost only three times, winning nineteen and tying seven.

Three days later came the New Year's Day Winter Classic against the Detroit Red Wings. The event was a sensation. Some 240,000 fans had applied for 41,000 seats. In the United States, the game was aired on NBC; in Canada, it was carried by the CBC and broadcast in both English and French.

The hype had risen to such levels that the families of the Detroit players flew to Chicago on a charter jet the day before. Adding to the festive atmosphere, the players wore vintage-style uniforms—the Red Wings donning a version of the sweaters worn by the 1928 Detroit Cougars, the Blackhawks a variation of their 1937 uniforms. For Hawks fans, the only downside was the final score, 6–4 in favor of the Red Wings.

The turnaround in the team's fortunes was enough to change the media's tune toward the Savard firing. "Four games into the season, McDonough and their wingmen did what all good leaders must," wrote columnist Dan McNeil. "They proved they were willing to be unpopular and fired one of the city's favorite sons. There was public outrage, of course, but with the Hawks winning nine of their last 10, the switch . . . was the right move."

The Blackhawks finished the regular season in second place in the Central Division with 104 points, good enough for the fourth overall seed in the Western Conference playoffs. It was the team's first postseason appearance since 2002—"unforgettable," is how the *Sun-Times* described the season, a campaign that "produced more lasting memories than perhaps the last 10 seasons combined."

The playoffs added yet more. The opening game was played in Chicago against the Calgary Flames, the Western Conference's fifth seed. The Hawks won in overtime and won again two days later after scoring three goals in the second period to overcome a two-goal deficit. They lost the next two in Calgary, then advanced after winning games five and six decisively, with Patrick Kane providing the winning goal in the clincher. The triumph marked the first time the Blackhawks had advanced to a conference semifinal since 1996.

And still the Hawks marched on, beating the Vancouver Canucks four games to two, the clincher a wild shootout in which Chicago scored three goals in under four minutes in the third period. For the first time in fourteen years, Chicago stood one series away from the Stanley Cup finals. The foe for the Western Conference championship, naturally, was a team that seemed to have had the Hawks' number all year—the Detroit Red Wings. And that didn't change. Detroit won the series four games to one, but the final outcome belied the closeness of the competition. Three of the five games were decided in overtime, including the final nail-biter on May 27 at Detroit's Joe Louis Arena, a spectacular goaltending exhibition that the Red Wings won 2–1 at 3:58 of the extra period.

The loss stung, of course, but the season was a smash success on virtually every level, starting with the most obvious, but most remarkable: for the first time in a long time, the Blackhawks were relevant again. And not just relevant, but a force—both in the city's sports landscape and as a national phenomenon.

Long gone were the rumblings over the firing of Savard, now safely in the fold as a team ambassador along with Hull, Mikita, and Tony Esposito. Virtually every change implemented by McDonough, with Wirtz's full support, could be found somewhere in the larger mosaic of the success the team was enjoying. Throughout, he had retained the friendly, open, call-me-Rocky, sit-with-the-fans approach. Anyone anticipating that a lurking semblance of his father might slip out in a moment of stress was mistaken.

For his part, Rocky was only slightly less than satisfied. It's said there are no moral victories in sport, only winning and losing. To celebrate coming close, that reasoning goes, is tantamount to blasphemy. Still, many fans sensed that the season just past was prelude. As the players cleared their lockers for the short off-season, they did so with hope.

Detroit would go on to lose the Stanley Cup that year to the Pittsburgh Penguins in seven games. Rocky almost immediately got back to work. But before he did, something struck him, a realization brought on by a surprise announcement involving his father. On the day the Blackhawks were eliminated, the Northwestern Memorial Foundation for Cancer Care and Research announced the creation of a foundation in the name of Bill Wirtz, who had left $19.5 million to seed a new program at Northwestern's Robert H. Lurie Center.

With the honoring of his father's name, Rocky realized that he had not had time to grieve, to really grieve, his father's death. He had shed tears, of course, but had been so consumed with his new responsibilities that there had been little time to reflect. When he did so now, it was with a single thought in mind: despite the cruelty Bill had shown Rocky toward the end of his life, for all of the anger Rocky had felt toward Bill, Rocky wished his father could see what was about to happen with the Blackhawks. For Rocky knew, somewhere down deep, that sometime in the near future was going to be *the* year. And Bill, who would have hated everything Rocky had done to turn that hunch into reality, would love it.

What It Feels Like to Be a Wirtz

The shot that ended the Blackhawks 2009 playoff run had barely trickled under the pads of goalie Cristobal Huet when Rocky's thoughts turned to an issue that had gnawed at him almost from the day he'd taken over the team: the suitability of Dale Tallon, the man largely responsible for putting together the team, as the general manager of the future.

To be sure, there was much to be proud of that spring as the players cleaned out their lockers and went their separate ways, some to nurse injuries, some home to their native Canada, some for R and R. Before the season began, Rocky had read the predictions—that the Hawks would likely make their first playoffs in years despite having the youngest team in the league, with players averaging twenty-five years old. But no one could have foreseen how far they'd get, advancing three rounds deep and—but for some inexperience and a couple of bad breaks—posing a legitimate threat to make it all the way to the Stanley Cup finals.

Rocky's postseason autopsy with McDonough revealed a bounty of other surprising achievements. Their forty-six wins were the most since the 1992–93 season—the last time the Hawks had made it to the finals. Their twenty-two road victories, always a good indicator of a team's poise and toughness, tied a team record.

The most jaw-dropping figure, however, applied to the fans. When Rocky had taken over the team less than two years earlier, attendance hunkered at twenty-ninth out of the league's thirty teams, just one spot above the cellar-dwelling Phoenix Coyotes. In 2009, the Hawks had catapulted to number one in attendance, beating out hockey-mad cities like Montreal, Detroit, and Philadelphia. In Chicago, the Hawks—not the Bears, Cubs, or Sox—were the hottest ticket in town just two years after barely registering in fan interest or media attention.

For Rocky, the *way* the franchise was reaching such heights provided the most gratifying aspect. The team was built on almost eerily prescient judgment and foresight. Every on-ice decision seemed the right decision. Every effort to reach alienated fans found the back of the net. Some critics, of course, had dismissed the moves as plucking low-hanging fruit. "What they didn't realize," McDonough says, "is that a lot of that fruit was cemented to the tree." The team had to beg to get the games on TV, he says, and prostrate itself before commissioner Gary Bettman to earn the rights to the Winter Classic.

The franchise itself, meanwhile, was more than efficient. It was likable. Rocky was the everyman who sat in the stands and cracked wise about past ignominy. McDonough was the marketing genius, smart and tough, with the great ideas. Toews was the earnest leader, Kane the baby-faced prodigy. As the second Blackhawks convention approached, people were starting to whisper the unthinkable—that the Blackhawks . . . the *B-l-a-c-k-h-a-w-k-s*—could actually go all the way.

Soon enough, though, turbulence began to buck the Hawks' smooth flight. The first bump came with a fumbling attempt to sign the team's MVP and top scorer, Martin Havlát, now a free agent. The negotiations, marred by pique and public sniping, took an especially bitter turn when the Hawks, after three months without progress, abruptly pulled all previously-discussed offers and tendered a take-it-or-leave-it one-year deal.

Havlát left it—and did so in exactly the kind of sour public way that neither Rocky nor McDonough wanted to see, one disturbingly reminiscent of the old days. Taking to Twitter on July 2, Havlát wrote, "Excited to be in Minny where I was welcomed and appreciated by management," and, "There's something to be said for loyalty and honor."

A few hours later, Havlát's agent, Allan Walsh, chimed in: "So much for taking care of the team MVP," he tweeted. "Havlát received multi-year offers from several teams . . . except Chicago. After 3 months of negotiating a long-term contract, Chicago would . . . not offer anything more than a 1 year deal."

In an interview, Havlát went on to accuse McDonough of undercutting Tallon out of petty jealousy. "My negotiation with Chicago was not between Dale and my agent. It was between Dale and McDonough," Havlát told TSN.ca. "Why? Because McDonough couldn't stand that Dale was so successful and getting the credit for building the Hawks from a last place team to making the Conference Final in three short years."

The charge was both petty and silly. Tallon had contributed to landing the team's better players, but McDonough—with Rocky's full backing—was the undisputed architect of the turnaround. Both McDonough and Rocky let it slide. Then again, they could afford to be charitable. The reason was that almost simultaneous to l'affaire de Havlát, Rocky signed off on a contract that landed a far more hotly pursued free agent. Marián Hossa was coming off a one-year deal with the Detroit Red Wings, the very team that had just eliminated the upstart Blackhawks. The veteran all-star had been the defensive anchor on virtually every team he had played for and he represented the one thing any team with serious aspirations for the ultimate prize desperately wanted: a great player with Stanley Cup experience.

Hossa had played in the last two Cup finals but lost, first with the Pittsburgh Penguins and then with the Red Wings. At age thirty, he had several good years left and his pick of teams, but he wanted to join the one he thought gave him the best chance at the championship that had eluded him. The Hawks' deal with Hossa was steep—$62.8 million over twelve years—but Rocky's willingness to pay it demonstrated in a dramatic way both his willingness to spend and his recognition that 2010 was the year to go all out.

Hossa's interest in the Blackhawks sent a potent message too. "This was a big deal," Rocky says. "He was the first player of elite caliber who ever sought us out, instead of us going after him. I think he saw something—the young players and the organization—that he really liked. He wanted to win a Cup badly and we were the team he chose."

With the Hossa signing, the team began to take on an air of inevitability, of destiny even. The fans were giddy, as were the owner and president—in public. Behind the facade, however, the two men worried.

There was a fissure in the foundation, they believed, that, while not apparent to those looking at the beautiful home they were building, could cause severe damage—if not now, then years down the line. And if there was one thing Rocky did *not* want, it was for the franchise to begin to sag and crumble because they'd neglected to address something fundamental.

Dale Tallon had been with the Blackhawks management for twenty years in a variety of positions, first as a director of player personnel, then as assistant general manager, and, starting in 2003, as general manager. Before that, coming to the Hawks to play center in 1973, he had had the misfortune of being perceived as the consolation prize for the disastrous Bobby Hull defection. Tallon even donned the Golden Jet's number 9 for one of the first preseason games, a move that provoked a torrent of boos so ferocious that the team immediately switched his number.

After his playing days, Tallon returned to the team as an announcer, a position he continued to hold over the years while he assumed various front office positions. During that time, he demonstrated to Bill the sole quality needed for longevity in the organization: unwavering loyalty.

Under Tallon, the team showed occasional promise but generally struggled, missing the playoffs year after year. Tallon scored a coup, however, in 2006. After another poor finish, the Blackhawks held the third pick in the draft. Tallon chose a gifted and mature eighteen-year-old Canadian named Jonathan Toews. The next year, with the first pick, Tallon scored again, taking Patrick Kane.

Through trades, free agency, and smart drafting, Tallon surrounded the two prodigies with a strong supporting cast, including Patrick Sharp, Kris Versteeg, and Brian Campbell. By the time of Bill's death in 2007, Tallon had built the nucleus of the team that had just fallen a series short of making the Stanley Cup finals in 2009.

But along with Tallon's successes, McDonough saw a number of things that troubled him. The only reason the Blackhawks drafted high enough to pick Toews and Kane was the failure of the years before. And that history of failure pointed to several fundamental problems. The first reflected the rapidly expanding responsibilities of a modern-day general manager. In the past it had been enough for a GM to hunt and sign players he thought could gel into winners within the confines of the owner's willingness to spend. The unsexy yet essential responsibilities crucial to the operations of a contemporary organization—staff issues, making contract deadlines, coordinating with the financial side of the company—occupied less time and were skills that were less valued.

In the last decade or so, however, the nature of the GM's job had changed. When it came to choosing players, for example, the practice had evolved from the traditional make-a-few-calls, watch-a-few-games, go-with-your gut approach. In hockey, as in other professional sports, the art of picking players had evolved to an analytics-based science that took into account virtually every moment and statistic connected to a player's career and coupled it with psychological profiles, input from experts around the league, and interviews with the player himself. The process started with a sophisticated team of scouts and a stocked farm system.

In Bill Wirtz's days running the Blackhawks, the GM's job was old-school. Bill employed only a handful of front office staff, a limited marketing or advertising department, and a skeleton sales team. He had about as much use for analytics as he did for postmodern poetry. Tallon fit into that world, Rocky and McDonough thought, but not the modern one of professional sports.

Some thought Tallon lacked a long-term strategy in his signings—giving little consideration to why a player was being signed, what he should be paid, and the length of his contract in the context of future teams.

At the same time, Tallon seemed to turn deliberate at the wrong moment. When McDonough and Tallon were discussing possible replacements for Denis Savard, Tallon had recommended Joel Quenneville. A great choice. The perfect choice, perhaps. But when it came time to act, Tallon hesitated. For appearance's sake, if nothing else, he wanted to give Savard at least ten games before firing him. The problem, says McDonough, was that "we had maybe a twenty- to twenty-four-hour window to get him. If we had waited, we would have lost him."

McDonough adds, "Now, it's true: there are people who said, and probably rightfully so, that, it wasn't fair to Denis Savard to fire him after only four games. Some columnists said, 'He had more loyalty to the Blackhawks than they had for him,' and they had a point. But this was one of those brutal decisions we knew we were going to have to make to get where we needed."

Tallon, McDonough says, "is a very, very, very, very good hockey guy, a very talented guy, and a very good guy. But as harsh as it sounds—and I know it does sound harsh—we weren't running a beauty contest here. I was given the task of hiring the absolute best people available, people who were good at every aspect of the position for which they were hired, people who I felt would give us the best opportunity to win going forward."

As it turned out, a mammoth blunder by Tallon that July, just days before the second Blackhawks convention, sealed his fate. One of the most basic duties of a hockey GM each year is to submit qualifying offers to the team's restricted free agents. The task is routine but crucial. Under league and players' union rules, submitting the offers limits the team's financial obligation—at most, the team must give a 10 percent raise to its restricted free agents, rather than bid against other teams on the open market. That summer, Tallon waited too long to send the offers to the league, potentially opening free agency to eight players, including Kris Versteeg, and ultimately costing the Blackhawks millions.

The money loss was bad enough. Worse in some ways was the PR hit. "Bumbling Hawks Re-sign Versteeg," read the banner over the *Sun-Times* July 9 story after the team eventually locked up the winger. Given the past—and the efforts they had made to change it—there couldn't have been a more triggering word to Rocky and McDonough than "bumbling."

Tallon apologized and signed all the free agents, though for significantly more than he would have paid but for the mistake. Days later, McDonough—with Rocky's blessing—announced that Tallon was being reassigned to a role as an executive advisor and the assistant

GM, Stan Bowman, son of the legendary former coach and front office executive Scotty Bowman, would take his place.

The blowback from both fans and the media was swift and savage. Tallon? The guy who drafted Kane, the previous year's rookie of the year, and Toews, the runner up? Savard was bad enough, but this . . .

The timing—just a few days before the second Blackhawks convention—made matters worse. "There were a lot of people that didn't want me to do that until the convention was over, so I could duck the criticism," McDonough recalls. "But I said, 'No way. If we're gonna do this, let's do it before. It's gonna be a tsunami on me, but let it rain, that's okay.' I wasn't going to hide behind the timing."

The storm indeed came. When McDonough was introduced at the opening ceremonies, he was booed for the first time in his career. Rocky, a sly grin curling a corner of his mouth, turned to his president and said, "Now you know what it feels like to be a Wirtz."

McDonough took the jibe in stride—until another controversy hit. The team revealed that its prized signing, Hossa, had a shoulder injury that would probably require surgery. If so, that would mean he would miss the first two months of the season, at least. What angered fans most was that the Blackhawks had known about the injury and the possible surgery when they announced his signing with great fanfare, but did not disclose it. When Bowman did, he severely underplayed the seriousness. Hossa had played with the injury throughout the postseason, the new GM explained, so the right winger might not have to have surgery. As it turned out, he did.

Then, as if the team needed more drama, its star player—the guy with the carefully crafted clean-cut image—got into the first of several scrapes with the law. On August 9, Patrick Kane was arrested and charged with felony robbery in his native Buffalo, New York, after an altercation with a taxi driver over twenty cents on the fare. The authorities said Kane grabbed and punched the driver. Kane apologized and the charges were later dropped, but it was another body blow for a franchise that had previously danced in the ring untouched.

The media let loose. "Welcome to the Bungle," the *Tribune* wrote. "The Blackhawks are one dragging-the-Stanley-Cup-through-the-UC-parking-lot step away from turning into the Yankees from 'Seinfeld.'"

Publicly, Rocky projected calm. The team's image had taken some dings, but not to worry. McDonough, too, downplayed any notion that his "hospital corners" team was devolving into old patterns. Every team, no matter how well run, has issues, they said. Privately, both men were upset. You simply couldn't make the mistake that Tallon did and suffer the PR gaffes that marked that off-season and pull off the miracle they were trying to execute. They hoped the worst had passed. Tallon was in a position better suited to him and they had full faith in Stan Bowman. Hossa's injury was a blow, but he *would* play.

As the long, difficult summer relinquished its hold, and the first chill of autumn rolled in like a refreshing Lake Michigan breeze, everything was in place. There weren't any guarantees. There never are. But if things went right, Rocky, McDonough, and the team that now bore their imprint stood on the cusp of pulling off perhaps the greatest turnaround in sports history.

What Just Happened?

The United Center had fallen dark. Small disks of light, beamed from long gauzy rods of luminous white, swept back and forth across the crowd, a moving sea of red and black. Just below, glistening and pristine, one end of the oval of ice changed colors under tinted light, gleaming purple, then red. On the other end, a laser rendering of the Blackhawks' Indian head logo spun slowly.

As the voice of the public announcer, Gene Honda, asked for the removal of hats, players from the opposing teams—the Colorado Avalanche in their traveling whites, the Blackhawks in their home reds—wheeled in lazy turns then drifted toward their own blue lines. They fell into rows, sticks resting on the surface, eyes cast upwards toward the American flag in spotlight in the rafters.

Earlier, four Blackhawks legends, Denis Savard, Stan Mikita, Tony Esposito, and Bobby Hull, all dressed in their old jerseys, had skated out, surprising and delighting the fans.

Now, tenor Jim Cornelison, standing in a tuxedo on a strip of red carpet emblazoned with the Blackhawks Indian head, raised a microphone. And then came the roar, rising fast and sweeping the arena. Thunderous, turbulent, it convulsed the space for one minute and thirty-eight seconds as Cornelison forged on, lashed by organist Frank Pellico to the last line: *O'er the laa-nd of the freeee . . . ROOOOAAAARRRR . . . and the home of the braaaaavee!!! ROOOOAAAARRRRR!!!!*

It was October 10, 2009, two years and two weeks from his father's passing, and Rocky Wirtz, having celebrated his fifty-eighth birthday five days earlier, stood with the rest of the twenty-thousand-plus fans. Somewhat more subdued than the others, he nonetheless smiled at all that he had seen and heard before settling into his familiar folding chair on the northeast concourse arc, just inside section 119.

This was the season home opener for the team he had sunk heart and soul into rescuing over the past two years, and that John McDonough had turned from a hapless, shoddily run, perennial loser into the seeming juggernaut circling the ice below. As he took his seat for the opening puck drop, what he had accomplished was fully on display. The Chicago Blackhawks were kings of the city's sporting world and, if things went the way he hoped, the team would be world champions for the first time since 1961.

The fans understood the potential. The tradition of cheering wildly throughout the national anthem had taken on a new intensity under Rocky's ownership—an emotional explosion that both fired the spirits and raised the pressure.

The game seesawed. The Hawks scored first, then the Avalanche netted the next two, then the Hawks evened it twenty-nine seconds later on a goal by John Madden, signed in the off-season. Colorado made it 3–2, then Chicago tied it. Finally, after nine rounds of shootouts—a club record—the Blackhawks won.

In a season that promised to be the most closely watched Blackhawks run since that last title—one that had come, as one writer pointed out, the year that Robert Frost read a poem at John F. Kennedy's inauguration—everyone seemed to be looking for signs and portents.

Winning the home opener—even in a record-setting way—seemed short of auspicious, a too-small sample from which to divine a greater destiny. Three days later, the team's second home game against the Calgary Flames appeared to justify the caution. The score before the first period had ended? The Flames up 5–0. Goalie Cristobal Huet was chased. His replacement, Antti Niemi, looked shaky. The fans jeered an easy puck stop by the new netminder and a seemingly meaningless score by the Hawks with a little over three minutes left in the period that put the score at 5–1.

Instead, the goal ignited an electrifying comeback. The Blackhawks tied the game in regulation and won it in overtime. It was the biggest comeback in team history (the previous record was from four down in 1926) and tied the NHL record. "It was crazy to come back like that," Patrick Kane told reporters after. "But what a fun game to be a part of." What shocked Rocky as much as the victory was what he saw when he glanced into the stands. No one had left after that disastrous first period. It was still far too early to believe in miracles, but that said something. It said a lot.

As the early weeks unfolded, Rocky continued overseeing each of the Wirtz Corporation's other businesses. He also had to cope with painfully arthritic knees—his doctors had recommended two replacements. Fine, Rocky had said, but not now. Starting with a 4–1 victory over the Los Angeles Kings on November 9 that kicked off an eight-game winning streak, Rocky found himself pulled deeper and deeper into what was rapidly growing into a phenomenon. Answering interview requests, entertaining clients, going to meetings, and simply attending games consumed most every waking hour.

"The Hawks haven't reached the mountaintop, not yet," wrote Carol Slezak in the *Sun-Times* in late January. "But they are getting closer to breathing the rare air of the Stanley Cup finals, and the rest of the league knows this. . . . It won't get any easier from here on out."

Game after game, Rocky hobbled into the United Center on his bum knees, stopping in at the Sonja Henie lounge to work the room before heading downstairs for dinner at the private Ketel One Club. Before his father's death, he could slip in almost unnoticed and dine in peace in the corner, unwelcome as he was at the family table where Bill held court with family and the honored guests of the evening—politicians, celebrities, visiting league officials. Now, with the deference paid an arriving sovereign, Rocky was ushered to that very table, where he wined and dined everyone from high rolling clients in the liquor business to close friends to bold-faced names from Chicago, New York, and Hollywood. Then he made his way through the mobs of well-wishers, stopping for every autograph, pausing for a few words with ushers, beer vendors, and security guards. Finally, he limped to his folding chair for another electrifying national anthem before another sellout crowd and, more often than not, another victory.

The jubilant, carnival atmosphere into which he stepped that season felt as surreal for him as it did the fans. Far from the Mausoleum on Madison, as the United Center had come to be known on those nights when a few thousand diehards jeered from the seats, the stadium seemed the center of the universe on game nights, an event, a happening. Fans of every stripe, most of them turned out in Blackhawks regalia, choked the concourse ringing the arena, lining up ten deep for beer and mustard-smeared brats and Frisbee-sized pretzels. Traffic around the building resembled the Kennedy Expressway at rush hour. Bars off nearby Ogden, Lake, and Madison Streets brimmed with pregame revelers. Old traditions, such as the team's fight song, "Here Come the Hawks," first introduced in 1968, were practiced with renewed vigor. New traditions—"Chelsea Dagger," a song released in 2006 by the Scottish band the Fratellis and adopted as the unofficial anthem after every Hawks score—shook the rafters nightly.

By that fall, according to *Forbes*, the estimated value of the Blackhawks franchise had risen by nearly a third since the previous season, from $205 million in 2008 to $300 million in 2010, the biggest increase among NHL teams during that span by far. Still, that was far from where Rocky wanted to be. Despite the leap, the Blackhawks ranked lowest in value among Original Six teams and a universe away from the most valuable franchise at the time—the $470 million Toronto Maple Leafs. At least the arrow was pointed up, a trend crystallized by attendance and TV ratings. A sellout streak had begun in the previous year's playoffs and showed no signs of abating, and Nielsen numbers had doubled over the year before for games telecast on Comcast SportsNet.

In short, Rocky and everyone else knew that things were good. Almost too good. In late November, on the eve of Thanksgiving, the Hawks won the first three games of a difficult road swing away from the United Center. The next game against the Western Conference–leading San Jose Sharks seemed to pose the season's biggest challenge, but it wasn't close. With Marián Hossa, the high-priced off-season acquisition playing his first game in a Blackhawks uniform, the team crushed the Sharks 7–2 as Hossa scored twice. *Tribune* beat reporter Chris Kuc wrote, the Hawks just "went from good to scary good. There's no doubt now. Chicago you have yourself a hockey team."

Behind the scenes, however, a variety of serious issues smoldered. Despite the vastly higher sums brought in by increased ticket sales, for example, the Hawks—unbeknownst to the public—ran out of money several times. Each shortage triggered a memo for another "capital call" from the parent company, Wirtz Corp., to cover operating expenses.

When such a request for cash was made after he took over in 2007, Rocky had hoped it would be a one-time thing. But building a contender, as he discovered, did not come cheaply. The reality, he realized, was that it would probably take another couple of years of continued sellouts and deep playoff runs for the team to be able to stand on its own. Still, Rocky knew the answer was not a return to his father's tactic of trying to cost-cut his way to success, a red line McDonough heartily seconded. "We're going to do everything we can to win," the president would later tell the *Tribune*. And that meant not going on the cheap—with anything. "We want this to be a destination for free agents," he said. "We want this to be a place where players want to play. We're going to charter our players to away games and we're going to stay in hotels that are going to be synonymous with a first-class operation."

Adding to Rocky's financial worries with the team was another behind-the-scenes aggravation—this one, Rocky believed, a petty jab thrown at him by Peter's lawyers. At issue was the disposition of a piece of Bill's will—a lucrative beer distributorship, Monarch Beverage Company, whose ownership was shared by Rocky and his four siblings. Peter's lawyers accused Rocky of shutting him out of decisions and failing to schedule shareholder meetings where complaints could be voiced. For the moment, it was just talk, but Rocky knew from the tone that the issue was not going to go away, as indeed it would not.

An even bigger obstacle loomed, however—one that Rocky and the rest of the front office dreaded and that had a direct bearing on the team. The Winter Olympics would be held in Vancouver in February, and the hockey tournament ranked as a featured event. The NHL encouraged players to participate, and that meant a seventeen-day break in the season during one of the most crucial periods in the drive to the playoffs.

For some NHL owners, those whose teams weren't contending for a playoff spot, lending out a player or two wasn't a big hardship. For Rocky, as the owner, it meant he was donating the services of six of his star players—Patrick Kane (playing for the United States), Jonathan Toews, Duncan Keith, and Brent Seabrook (Canada), and Marián Hossa and Tomáš Kopecký (Slovakia). The Olympic competition would be every bit as intense, if not more so, than the NHL regular season. The big worry was not just injury, but also exhaustion, burnout, and the loss of momentum. The Hawks, after all, were riding a four-game winning streak after edging the Columbus Blue Jackets 5–4 on February 14, the last game before the break. When they returned there would be a twenty-one-game sprint to the finish. Get off to a sluggish start and who knew how bad it could get?

Like all NHL owners, Rocky fell under a strict no-comment edict, but privately he was dismayed. No one could argue that the Olympic tournament wasn't thrilling. The Canadians won the gold medal in the championship game by beating the U.S. team in overtime on a goal by Pittsburgh Penguins star Sidney Crosby. But for a team like the Blackhawks, seriously pressing to win its first Stanley Cup in forever, it was a physically and emotionally draining distraction at the worst time. For those who played, that is. For the other seventeen team members, it was a spring vacation, which meant they had to get back in gear after a long layoff. (The NHL no longer allows its players to participate.)

Fortunately, the Blackhawks escaped the games without serious injury. But executives watched their team slump in March, suffering two three-game losing streaks. Worse, one of the crucial defensive cogs, Brian Campbell, went down with a broken rib and collarbone after a hard shove that many considered a cheap shot by Alex Ovechkin of the Washington Capitals. Campbell, a vital piece of the Blackhawks defense, would be out several weeks and it was uncertain—doubtful even—that he could heal in time for the playoffs.

At around the same time, the organization had to deal with another controversy involving Patrick Kane. This time, the incident also involved two other Blackhawk stars, Kris Versteeg and John Madden. In late January, the *Vancouver Province's Orland Kurtenblog* ran four photos of the trio shirtless in a limousine with three women.

Behind the scenes, Rocky, McDonough, and Bowman felt the kerfuffle that followed hardly rose to the level of scandal and certainly didn't call for any discipline. But with the photos splashed all over the Vancouver papers, the team had to make some kind of response. The organization issued a mild rebuke. Rocky, following the advice of McDonough, remained mum. All were confident the incident would blow over, and it did. The players, meanwhile, contacted Rocky to apologize. Versteeg called to say he was sorry. "What he said was, 'I would never want to do anything to hurt the team,'" Rocky recalls. "I told him he was fine, there was nothing to apologize for, but that he should be careful about putting himself in potentially embarrassing positions." With the Hawks increasingly seen as favorites to make it to the Stanley Cup finals, they were going to be under intense scrutiny, especially in rival cities such as Vancouver.

More worrisome, as the regular season's end approached, was the Hawks' continuing poor play. In the last weeks of March, the team lost seven out of ten games. "They appear to be falling apart," Carol Slezak wrote in the *Sun-Times*. The Hawks had suffered through a similar late-season slump the previous year, at one point losing five in a row, but this was a deeper, more experienced team, and the expectations amplified the slightest off note into a symphony of fretting.

Rocky knew better than to panic—in an eighty-two-game season, there were bound to be slumps. But he was worried. "You have doubts. The players have doubts. You don't know what's going to happen."

The players were saying the right things—that is, not making excuses. And Joel Quenneville rewarded the faith his bosses had placed in him. After the second loss in a row against the lowly Columbus Blue Jackets, the head coach ran a special practice drill requiring players to fight for the puck in the corners—"battle drills," he called them. The tactic seemed to shake the players from their doldrums.

The team immediately found its form again, reeling off six straight wins. Entering the last game of the season, they merely needed a victory against Detroit to finish first in the conference. They fell just short, however, losing 3–2 and ceding the Western Conference's top seed to San Jose.

Still, by nearly every measure, the regular season had met or surpassed the high expectations that had pressed in on the franchise since the loss to Detroit in the previous year's playoffs. The team won fifty-two games, a franchise record. The Hawks finished with 112 points, another club best. And Chicago set a team record for most road wins, twenty-three. Now, they were about to begin the playoffs for the second year in a row—a milestone they hadn't reached in more than twenty years. What's more, they were not just contenders to make the Stanley Cup finals, but favorites.

For Rocky, and the tens of thousands of fans now regularly packing the United Center, the position was astonishing, wonderful—and nerve-wracking. The unspoken but deeply felt understanding was that anything short of a championship would be a disappointment. More than that—it would be a crushing blow. The team's turnaround had given the fans a great gift, but the success carried with it a great burden: hope.

Rocky carried his own hopes and burdens. He was still largely estranged from his sisters and completely estranged from his brother, Peter. The two only spoke through their attorneys. Peter did not come to a single game all year, and if his sisters did, they scrupulously avoided any encounters with Rocky. The Blackhawks franchise had increased in value by hundreds of millions of dollars. The liquor company's sales, meanwhile—$350 million in 2007—had likewise exploded, now topping more than a billion dollars a year. Why not embrace the success? Enjoy it? The siblings had not offered as much as a simple thank-you. God only knew what their reaction would be if the team didn't win the championship everyone was predicting.

Meanwhile, there was the matter of his father and grandfather. Rocky didn't believe in ghosts, but as the team that Bill and Arthur had ruled for more than a half century entered the 2010 playoffs, he felt their presence in every corner, in every moment. Of course, he had no time to dwell on these deeply felt family matters. The playoffs were beginning. His team had a championship to win and if his own brother and sisters scorned it—and him—by God, the city was giving the Wirtz name a second chance. If they won.

The first hurdle was the team from Nashville. The Predators were a fierce, physical, disciplined outfit. No matter how they fared during the regular season, the team seemed to find a way to bloody and occasionally beat their postseason opponents. Sometimes both.

The 2010 version was no different. The Preds had finished with a respectable 100 points, but in the high-flying Western Conference that was good enough only for a seventh seed. In six games between Nashville and Chicago during the regular season, the Blackhawks had won four. Accordingly, they were heavy favorites. Still, there were questions. Antti Niemi, a rookie, had been the team's starting goalie since January, when he had replaced the faltering Cristobal Huet. Niemi had played great—at times, inspired—but the playoffs were a different matter. Teams skated faster and hit harder, no unit more so than Nashville. The Blackhawks were still missing Brian Campbell, and in the last third of the season their power play had been anemic at best.

The series opened at the United Center on April 16 with the sort of pregame spectacular that had made the arena one of the NHL's loudest and most raucous venues. As usual, Rocky took his folding chair after the national anthem roar and settled in nervously for the opening face-off.

If he'd harbored doubts before this night, he was joined by the rest of the city after it. Chicago lost the first game 4–1. The Hawks evened the series two nights later 2–0, Niemi's shutout having seemingly restored order. When the series moved to Nashville, however, the Predators swamped the Hawks again, the 4–1 score a repeat of the first game. Being down two games to one was hardly insurmountable, and the Hawks got a lift when Brian Campbell, still not fully healed from the broken collarbone he suffered in mid-March, decided to play. Chicago again bounced back behind Niemi's second shutout.

In game five, widely considered the pivotal point in the series, the Predators looked well on their way to putting the Hawks on the brink. The team was down a goal, 4–3, late in the third period and shorthanded due to a major penalty on Marián Hossa. The seconds ticked away . . . 30 . . . 20 . . . and then with 13.6 seconds left, the Hawks pulled off a miracle. Kane scored the tying goal, creating bedlam at the UC. They completed the comeback at 4:07 of overtime, after Hossa, jumping onto the ice after his penalty, swept in with the puck and launched the game winner. Two days later, on April 26, the Hawks put the Predators away with a 5–3 victory.

Next up was Vancouver, with whom the Hawks had developed a chippy rivalry in recent years, pushing, shoving, talking trash. Once again, the Hawks lost the first game to the Canucks by the disappointing count of 5–1. Chicago came right back, however, and after giving up one more game to Vancouver, closed the series out on May 11 with a payback 5–1 win.

If the regular season was any indication, the Western Conference finals, against the San Jose Sharks, should have been the toughest. After all, the Sharks had leapfrogged the Hawks on the last day for best regular-season record and top seed. But Chicago won the first two games in San Jose, and, back at the United Center, won again in overtime. Game four was a mere formality. The Hawks won 4–2, advancing to the Stanley Cup finals for the first time since 1992—the year they had been swept by the Pittsburgh Penguins, the closest Bill would ever come to winning it all. That year marked the beginning of the team's long, slow death spiral.

This time, the Hawks opponent looked like no match. The Philadelphia Flyers had finished the regular season with eighty-eight points—a full two dozen fewer than the Blackhawks—and had barely qualified for the playoffs. The battle for the final Eastern Conference postseason spot came down to the last game of the season, an overtime thriller between the Flyers and the New York Rangers. The Flyers won in a shootout to squeak in as a seventh seed.

But in the NHL, teams can get hot at exactly the right time. That was the Flyers' story. First they beat their rival New Jersey Devils, then the Boston Bruins, and then the Montreal Canadiens.

The Hawks-Flyers series opened on June 10 at the United Center. Everything—the noise, the anthem, the traffic-choked streets outside, the vendors crawling the neighborhood, the packed bars, the watch parties, the sports reports leading the evening news—all of it merged into one giant cable jolt of electricity that blasted through the city like bolts from a lightning storm.

Rocky had rarely experienced nerves over his team and he tried not to show them now as he took his habitual seat in the folding chair in section 119. He wore his usual understated suit and tie, trying as best as he could to maintain the same routine he had maintained throughout the regular season and playoffs—though in certain ways that was impossible. Reporters from all over the world had descended on the United Center, and all of them, it seemed, wanted to interview the man behind the miracle.

When the game started, however, it was just Rocky, twenty-thousand-plus fans, and the game. That contest turned into a scoring fest, with leads switching back and forth several times—"shootout at the OK Corral," the coach, Quenneville, called it. The teams combined for eleven goals—six for the Blackhawks, five for Philadelphia.

The second game was the first's opposite. Blackhawks goalie Antti Niemi made fifteen saves in the second period and fourteen in the third, many of them spectacular, to give the Blackhawks a 2–0 lead in the best-of-seven series.

Whispers that the Hawks were going to sweep filtered up to Rocky, who shook his head. "Let's not get ahead of ourselves," he said. He was right. The Flyers took game three in overtime, 4–3, sending another type of jolt—of anxiety—shooting through the city.

"Uh-oh. I think I heard the entire city of Chicago make that sound," wrote Rick Telander in the *Sun-Times*. "Uh-oh, as in, You mean, the Blackhawks aren't going to sweep these losers from Philly?

"Uh-oh, as in, Get beat tonight at the Wachovia Center and it's a .500 Stanley Cup series?

"Uh-oh, as in, Remember the 2003 playoff Cubs?

"Like crabgrass, hockey doubt has appeared in our town."

The weeds spread with game four, when the Flyers did indeed even the series with a 5–3 win. Feeding the worry was the emergence of a villain. At six feet, six inches tall and 220 pounds, with a high forehead and a face whose expression alternated between fierce and cocky, Chris Pronger had dominated the Hawks' top line of Kane, Toews, and Dustin Byfuglien (pronounced BUFF-linn) in

Philadelphia's two wins, shoving opponents, playing keep-away with the puck after the whistle, glowering in the faces of the Hawks. At the United Center fans booed and jeered every time he touched the puck.

In game five they began chanting his name when Byfuglien took his revenge with a crushing hit on the defenseman. "Proonnngeeer-rrr! Proonnngeerrr!" The Hawks as a whole got payback, too, scoring a flurry of goals on their way to a 7–4 victory and reaching the brink of hoisting the Stanley Cup.

Game six took place on June 9 at the Wachovia Center in Philadelphia. Long before this series, the City of Brotherly Love had earned a reputation for having some of the rowdiest, most boorish, roughest fans, a distinction in which the city seemed to take a perverse pride. Philadelphia Eagles fans famously booed Santa Claus and put the Washington Redskins mascot, an amiable retired car salesman, in the hospital with a broken leg.

Incidents had marred the two previous games in Philadelphia, both of which the Flyers had won. "Hawks fans were getting beaten up in the bathrooms, outside the arena," Rocky says. At one point, Flyers fans discovered the hotel where the Hawks players were staying and were planning to storm the place, the team's security warned. The Hawks owner says state police told him before game six that "they could not guarantee the safety" of any fan wearing Blackhawks gear in the Philadelphia stands.

As the Blackhawks bus pulled into the arena's parking lot to unload the players, a group of fans swarmed the vehicle, rocking it from side to side.

Rocky refused to talk about the possibility of winning that night. The traditional preparations—champagne, championship T-shirts, caps—were handled by McDonough. Rocky did take his president's suggestion that the team fly in the families of the players and staff, chartering a 737 to bring in dozens of loved ones.

As the game progressed, a low-scoring, tightly played nail-biter, Rocky could hide his anxiety no longer. Several times, recalls Chipparoni, Rocky and McDonough "would go to the back of the suite, away from the TVs. I've never seen them that nervous. They were pacing like expectant fathers."

Regulation ended in a 3–3 tie. For McDonough, who had suffered through close calls with the Cubs only to see them collapse in the end, the tie in regulation was torturous. "All I could think of was, 'Here we go again,'" he says. "Man, I've been here before and it didn't turn out well." Rocky tried to mingle during the break before the overtime period, but he struggled. "I just couldn't let myself think, 'What if,'" he says. "I couldn't go there. Because if you lose . . ."

Overtime began with the teams streaking back and forth across the ice. The crowd stood, roaring any time the Flyers came remotely close to the Hawks' goal. At about four minutes into the extra period, something strange happened. With the Hawks swarming the Philadelphia zone, Brian Campbell took the puck to the blue line, then dropped it off to Kane. The winger faked left, then right, skating around the Flyers defenseman, and then, almost parallel with the Philadelphia goal, snapped a shot with a snake-strike wrist flick. The puck disappeared. "Time stopped," McDonough recalls.

The crowd stood in confused silence, then began to rumble when they saw Kane shed his gloves and rocket down the ice, several Blackhawks in tow. Other players leapt off the bench and joined a mob at the Blackhawks' end, jumping into the arms of Niemi. Quenneville remained on the bench with his arms around his assistants.

Far above, in his upstairs suite, Rocky saw what had happened. The puck had slipped under the pads of Flyers goalie Michael Leighton and lodged out-of-sight beneath part of the netting. Rocky looked over at McDonough, who looked back at him and shrugged as if to say, "What just happened?" Rocky broke into a grin.

"I think," Rocky said, "that we just won the frickin' Stanley Cup."

The Breakaway

He knew. All around him people gaped—in the plushness of the sky suite, in the stunned bowl of fans, on the ice itself, where the Flyers players looked confused, in bars on Broad Street and 768 miles away along Madison—thousands, millions maybe, stared. They weren't sure. He was.

Rocky had seen it on a flat screen suspended to his right, an NBC feed without a delay. The puck had darted under the goalie's mitt, then skittered under a fold of padding like a mouse diving for cover. The Flyer's goalie, Michael Leighton, looked into his empty glove, absently flapping it open and shut, hoping the puck had somehow stuck in the webbing. The fans stood in stunned silence.

The confirmation came moments later, the flat monotone of the words echoing through the Philadelphia arena like a gate announcement at a bus stop. "Blackhawks goal scored by Patrick Kane . . . at 4:06, assisted by . . ."

Things moved quickly now. Rocky, Marilyn, and Marilyn's daughter, Elizabeth, along with a group including members of the team's leadership—McDonough, his right-hand man Jay Blunk, and other executives—joined Rocky's son, Danny, and his wife, Anne, and Rocky's two daughters, Hillary and Kendall—in a rush down a hallway to a private elevator that would take them to ice level for the Stanley Cup presentation ceremony.

As the Blackhawks brass crowded into the elevator, Rocky shot a glance at McDonough, who laughed quietly. When the door opened, the group was escorted through the Hawks locker room and out onto the ice. There, glinting under the bright lights, polished to such a sheen that it glimmered like a small star, rose the grail his father had chased unsuccessfully for forty-nine years. The Stanley Cup, in all its silver glory, displayed on a strip of red carpet set upon a table.

By now, dozens of television and print media from all over the world were making their way around the ice, sticking mikes in faces, scribbling on pads, while families of the players and folks from the front office poured onto the rink in wonderstruck awe. Jonathan Toews, winner of the Conn Smythe trophy for most valuable player in the postseason, hoisted the Cup first, and was followed by one player after another—Patrick Kane, Patrick Sharp. Duncan Keith's smile gaped from the seven teeth he had lost in the series clincher against the San Jose Sharks. The entire team skated around the rink in triumph. "Give the Cup to Rocky!" Toews shouted. Dressed in his customary sober suit and subdued tie, bum knees and all, Rocky heaved the thirty-five-pound trophy over his head and beamed as friends, family, and fans who had drifted down to the area cheered.

Because the win had occurred on Philadelphia's ice, the few diehard Flyers fans who stayed behind did their best to sully the moment, booing loudly, but by now, with far more Hawks fans having migrated toward the ice, the Flyers faithful where overwhelmed by chants of "Rock-y! Rock-y!"

Interviewed in the moment, Rocky admitted what he only now could publicly acknowledge: When Kane's shot found the net, "It was like the weight of the world was lifted from my shoulders," he said. "I didn't know if we could bring the Cup back to Chicago."

Despite all that had passed before, Rocky dedicated the win to his father, his grandfather, and his uncle, Michael. "They worked their asses off for so long" trying to be in the position he was in now, he said. As a final full-circle gesture, completely unplanned, he handed the Cup to the younger man smiling beside him: his son, Danny.

After the obligatory champagne and beer showers in the locker room—and in the case of coach Quenneville, a cigar—the team boarded a chartered jet back to Chicago. Before Rocky left the

Wachovia Center, he paused as he passed a small room just off the team's clubhouse. There, sitting alone in front of a laptop, was Scotty Bowman, father of Stan, a senior advisor to the Blackhawks, and already a legendary figure in the NHL. With the victory that night, Bowman now claimed a role in eleven Stanley Cup championships. And yet, rather than join in the champagne showers, he found a room and replayed each goal again and again. Rocky just shook his head and, with friends and family, boarded a private jet for the flight home.

The players, bleary-eyed and reeking of beer and bubbly, landed shortly before four A.M. at a private terminal at O'Hare International Airport, the aircraft taxiing in through giant arcs of water gushing from fire trucks positioned on the tarmac. As the plane slowed to a halt the pilot's window popped open and a long red-and-black Hawks banner flowed out. Jonathan Toews emerged with the Cup overhead as the players, now in dark suits and ties, pumped fists and yelled their way down the stairs and into the terminal. From O'Hare, they immediately embarked on a pub crawl, stopping first at Harry Caray's restaurant in Rosemont, then on to the Pony Inn on Belmont as bouncers held back screaming fans.

For Rocky, intruding on his players' gloriously raucous celebration was the last thing he wanted to do. After granting countless interviews, spending most of the night clutched with anxiety, fending off the presence of the ghosts of his father and grandfather—after three years of effort to get to this place, he was exhausted.

The weariness smacked him on the plane ride home. "We were still wet from the champagne," he recalls, "and the air was very cold—not that we were complaining. You're just so relieved and so happy. The stress of an overtime game, the winning goal having to be reviewed. It was a lot." A cheer arose when Rocky's pal, John Miller, lifted a bottle of champagne for a toast on the way home—until it was noted that he'd only brought one bottle. "That's great for me," Rocky quipped. "But what about the rest of us?"

The jet set down at three A.M. at Palwaukee Municipal Airport (now Chicago Executive Airport) in Wheeling, a three-runway airfield about eighteen miles northwest of the city where Rocky's players, Cup in hand, were about to party through the dawn. The plane taxied anonymously to the small terminal, where a small group of friends, headed by Bruce Wirtz MacArthur, stood waiting with more champagne.

Rocky and Marilyn walked unrecognized to their car in the humid June night, just another businessman and his spouse back from a routine trip. They arrived to their house in Kenilworth about a half hour later. Rocky was grateful there were no surprises. "I just wanted a shower," he recalls. He struggled to unknot his tie—"Have you ever tried to take off a tie when it's wet?" Finally, he stood under the hot shower. As the town partied into the early hours of the morning, Rocky and Marilyn settled onto a couch and turned on the TV, hoping to catch some overnight highlights. They drifted off instead, the screen still flickering.

• • •

By Friday, two days later, Rocky had recharged himself, so that he now stood on the top platform of a double-decker bus at the corner of Canal and Washington. Players, families, and other Hawks executives joined him on the sunny summer morning, the heat already making Rocky wish he'd been warned that no one would be wearing sport coats. A line of accompanying buses idled in preparation for the day's event, the biggest party yet for the triumphant Hawks: a tickertape parade. Everyone who had anything remotely to do with the team had already arrived, invited to ride in the bus caravan. To Rocky's surprise, his three sisters, Gail, Karey, and Alison, had showed up and climbed aboard another bus. Peter did not appear.

Mercifully, someone produced a short sleeve shirt for Rocky, who quickly shed his blazer. The route would take them through side streets, winding up at the corner of Michigan and Wacker, where a podium had been erected for speeches. No one knew what to expect. "You heard about six hundred thousand people when the Bears won [in 1986], but we had no idea how many people were going to show up."

The first hint came as the buses rolled out on their winding journey. "On every street, every cross street, you weren't seeing people ten deep," Rocky recalls. "You were seeing people fifty, sixty, seventy deep." People waved from rooftops. Some clung to street lamps.

When the buses turned onto Michigan, the crowd—later estimated as high as two million—broke through police barriers and nearly engulfed the motorcade.

Mounting the podium at Michigan and Wacker, a perch that overlooked the nexus of the city's bustling Loop, Rocky stood awestruck. Before him, shoulder to shoulder in the heat, rippled a roiling sea of black and red. Fathers in newly-bought championship caps boosted daughters and sons onto their shoulders. Downtown workers by the thousands waved out of windows, flinging out strands of paper. A few of the more intrepid climbed onto bridge stanchions and light poles, one man peeling off his shirt and swinging it like a rally towel. Despite the heat, most of the crowd dressed in Blackhawks jerseys, roaring as the players were introduced. A few fans came dressed as a Stanley Cup. Others hoisted homemade replicas. One man worked in true Chicago fashion: he arrived wearing a beer keg costume that he'd spray-painted silver, sporting a similarly painted top hat crowned with a silver salad bowl.

A few years earlier, barely six thousand glum souls clomped down the United Center stairs and into their seats to watch another dreary Blackhawks performance, another loss, cursing the team, the players, and, most often, the Wirtz name as they filed back out. On this sweltering June morning, the two million fans—old and new—stood like carolers at a Christmas outing, looking up into a paper blizzard of red, white, and black.

When the ceremony began, Mayor Richard M. Daley took to the mike. "BOOOOOoooooo!!!!!!!" He was followed by Governor Pat Quinn. "BOOOooooooo!!!!!!!"

("Not a good day to be a politician," Rocky says.) Then came the players, including the toothless Duncan Keith, asking if anyone knew a good dentist. And, of course, Rocky, and the ever-present chant.

"Two and a half years ago, we stood before you and committed that the Chicago Blackhawks would be a relevant team again," Rocky said, his voice echoing out across the waves of roaring fans. "We also said we would not rest until we brought the Stanley Cup home to you. Well, if this ain't relevant, I don't know what is!"

Afterwards, some two thousand friends, family, and Wirtz business clients were feted at the Hyatt, the Cup the only centerpiece needed.

Rocky had little time to bask, however. Four days later, he checked himself into Northwestern Memorial Hospital for his long-neglected knee surgery. He started with the right so that he could drive as soon as possible. Six weeks later, he had the left replaced. By August, he was feeling better. His joints still ached, but nothing was going to keep him from sharing the Cup with one particularly special person.

He traveled to Springfield, the Cup in tow, on August 19, ostensibly to celebrate the victory at the State Capitol. The trophy gleamed in the Rotunda, in the Executive Mansion, and on the Illinois State Fairgrounds. Rocky's deeper purpose, however, was to grant the trophy a personal audience with the closest person to royalty in the Wirtz family: his Aunt Betty. Until Rocky had taken over, Bill's sister, the last surviving direct descendent of Arthur, had lived a quiet life. "No one cared about the Blackhawks down there," Rocky says. "You'd never see a jersey." With the turnaround, however, the logo was everywhere, particularly when the town realized that Betty Wirtz, who had been present in Detroit the last time the Hawks had won the Cup in 1961, had called the city home for years.

Rocky brought her to the Executive Mansion as his special guest for a luncheon with Illinois Governor Pat Quinn and others. In that gathering, Rocky was delighted to note that she was not referred to as Rocky's Aunt, but instead *he* was referred to as Betty's nephew. "He was so kind to bring the Cup here," she says. "It was a wonderful moment for me and the city."

Around then, though, a lingering predicament resurfaced. Rocky received a call from attorneys representing Peter. The brother would be filing a lawsuit against Rocky over the Monarch beer distributorship. For complex reasons, the company had been set up by Bill and Arthur as separate from other Wirtz holdings. By 2010, Rocky owned 51 percent, and the five siblings shared the remaining 49 percent.

A week before the new season began, Peter hauled his brother into court, accusing Rocky of undervaluing the siblings' share in the beer company and withholding the information that would prove it. A month after Peter filed the lawsuit, his sisters Gail, Karey, and Alison joined the action.

Rocky denied undervaluing the shares and insisted that he had furnished all relevant information. The suit itself pained him deeply.

Rocky believed he had done nothing but fatten the coffers of every family member. And to go public with the family dispute just days before the Blackhawks were about to raise the championship banner at the United Center struck Rocky as extremely petty.

The parties eventually settled the suit—the terms undisclosed. Capitulating to a request from his sisters ("they were trying everything they could to get us back together," Rocky says), Rocky offered Peter a director's chair on the Wirtz Corp. board, a position that would have allowed him to ask questions and have proprietary access to the company books. It was a plum that neither Bill nor Arthur ever offered to Peter. Rocky did so, he says, because "I was trying to give him an olive branch."

Peter turned it down, and in doing so gave up a last chance to be a part of the family business his grandfather and father had built from nothing. He was likewise crushing any hope of reconciliation with his older brother along with most any chance of rejoining the franchise he had once professed to love so dearly.

• • •

On Saturday, October 9, 2010, none of that mattered. Certainly not to the 22,161 fans packed into the United Center, and not even to Rocky. This was no ordinary home opener and it would provide no ordinary opening night ceremony.

Rocky knew what was coming—could feel it like the approach of a cleansing rain. The first roar erupted when the lights went down. Camera phone flashes lit up the giant bowl like an explosion of stars. Highlight images of the championship season flared on the Jumbotron overhead and then on the ice itself, turning the surface into a giant, gleaming movie screen. All the triumphs and tough moments swept by in a stirring blur, scored by an orchestral version of U2's "With or Without You."

From one end of the ice, captain Jonathan Toews emerged holding the Stanley Cup over his head. He skated to center ice, tracked by three spotlights, and placed it on a white table. He patted the trophy three times before skating off, giving way to five members of the 1961 championship team, including Bobby Hull, Stan Mikita, Pierre Pilote, Eric Nesterenko, and Ab McDonald. The group unfurled a large white banner bearing the words CHICAGO BLACKHAWKS, STANLEY CUP CHAMPIONS, 2010. The old handed off the banner to the new—members of the 2010 Stanley Cup team. The banner, attached to hooks, then began to rise slowly while the players shook hands and patted each other on the back.

In the years to follow, the ceremony would be repeated two more times—in 2013 and 2015. Both thrilling runs, amazing seasons, full of more moments added to the team's lore: The triple overtime win in game one against the Boston Bruins, another Original Six team, in 2013. Game six of that series, when Dave Bolland's winning goal came with less than a minute left in the game, the latest a championship-deciding goal had ever been scored in Cup play. The 2015 clinching game, a 2–0 shutout of the Tampa Bay Lightning, when the Hawks won the Cup on its home ice for the first time since 1938—in the process collecting their third winner's trophy in six years.

The "D" word—dynasty—appeared in full glory on the cover of the June 16, 2015, edition of *Sports Illustrated*:

MODERN DYNASTY

THE BLACKHAWKS

6 SEASONS / 3 CUPS / 1 MODEL FRANCHISE

• • •

The break from the past found expression in more than trophies. Ten years after Rocky took over, the team value had skyrocketed from $168 million in 2006 to $925 million in 2016. As of April 2017, the team boasted a sellout streak of 414 games—352 regular season and 62 postseason—on the way to leading the NHL in attendance for the ninth consecutive season.

Since the beginning of Rocky's tenure, the season ticket holder base in 2017 had increased 300 percent and the team's TV ratings nearly 500 percent.

Championships are the thing, though—even for a businessman like Rocky. But how do you choose among your children—2010, 2013, 2015?

For him, the answer is easy and it came that night in October 2010, when the championship banner began its slow ascent to the rafters. As he stepped to the microphone to address the crowd, he couldn't help but think back to an evening three years and three days earlier, when the crowd booed his father's memory. They chanted Rocky's name in unison now—the awful, fraught times forgiven. Bill's children had wept out of hurt and humiliation that earlier night. On this evening, Rocky's son, Danny, stood before his Dad's habitual folding chair on the concourse and wept too—in his case, out of pride. "Hearing him being announced and then twenty-two thousand people chanting 'Rocky'? I just couldn't hold it back," the son—and heir—says. "To hear how the fans adored what he did, what he accomplished, give him the chants and the support. It was as if everything had come full circle." Rocky himself, rarely one to reveal his emotions, choked up as well. For three years now, fans had stopped Rocky—on the streets, in bars, on his way to his seat among them in the United Center, where, like them, he lived and died with each goal—to express their gratitude.

When Rocky, in his sober suit and tie, stepped to the mike that night, marveling for the thousandth time that he—a Wirtz—was being cheered, not booed, it was his turn.

"Thank you," he said to the crowd three times, a hat trick, the champagne toast to a heart-stirring breakaway.

Acknowledgments

The genesis of this book reaches back to 2008 and an article I wrote for *Chicago* magazine, where I have been a senior writer for some fifteen years. Like much of the city, even those who cared not a whit about hockey, I followed the astonishing turnaround of its beloved Blackhawks with a mix of awe and fascination—awe at what can happen when the exact right person takes the reins of a struggling concern, be it sports franchise, business, or anything, really, in the exact right moment, and picks the exact right people to execute a vision. When Rocky Wirtz took over the Blackhawks in 2007 after the death of his father, the legendary, larger-than-life, defiantly irascible Bill Wirtz, the franchise arguably languished at the lowest point of its existence. Bill Wirtz, fairly or not, was one of the most despised owners in sport. The franchise itself had been named by ESPN as not just the worst hockey organization, but the worst *in all of professional athletics*. Some hope flickered when it became clear Rocky would be running the show, but no one was expecting miracles. Rocky, and the team he assembled—most notably, John McDonough, the former Cubs marketing savant whom Rocky pried away from what McDonough at the time believed was his dream job—gave them just that: three Stanley Cup championships in less than ten years.

Publicly, at least, the team's resurrection seemed almost fated, its rise from laughingstock to dynasty an uninterrupted series of triumphs. The moves Rocky and McDonough made seemed so obvious in retrospect that some brushed them off as what any fairly competent ownership team would have done.

Having researched the *Chicago* magazine piece, however, I knew better, which is where the fascination came in. Throughout the Hawks' rise, occasional hints at family discord had surfaced—as had reports of the financial troubles the franchise faced. But virtually no one beyond the innermost circle had the slightest notion of the magnitude of the family struggle that had gone on behind the scenes in Bill Wirtz's last years, or in the period immediately following his death. It was clear, yes, that in making the wholesale changes, Rocky was going against virtually every principle his father held dear. Not known was that Bill had effectively excommunicated his son from anything to do with the Blackhawks, conferring almost all his attention on Rocky's brother, Peter. The wounds of that family struggle have yet to fully heal and, in the case of Rocky and Peter, may never.

To this day, Rocky and Peter do not speak other than through their attorneys. Rocky's relationship with his other siblings, Gail, Karen (Karey), and Alison, has improved, but is still strained.

None of Rocky's siblings agreed to participate in the writing of *The Breakaway*.

I am deeply grateful to those others who did—especially Rocky himself—for without them, of course, there would be no book. One of the things that struck me when I embarked on this project was Rocky's insistence that it in no way be a hagiography—and certainly not a vanity project of the sort that owners and captains of industry often prefer, nay demand, be written about them. To that end, he was candid in the extreme—wincingly so, at times, even for a journalist like me who relies on sources' willingness to expose warts. Rocky prevailed upon most all of the other key figures in the book, including John McDonough, to share honestly.

I thank them all.

But far more people than those one interviews go into the making of such a project, so I owe much gratitude to Richard Babcock, my editor, mentor, and friend—a distinguished author in his own right—who talked me off the metaphorical ledge many times during the writing, to say nothing of the outstanding guidance he provided at every turn. Thank you to Enrica Aldini, who provided invaluable help as my research assistant. I'd like to extend special thanks as well to Guy Chipparoni, the Chicago Blackhawks, copy editor Dan Lindstrom, and the editorial team at Northwestern University.

Chicago magazine's publisher and editor, Susanna Homan, and executive editor, Terry Noland, graciously agreed to give me a leave of absence of several months, without which I never would have reached the finish line. They also granted permission for the use of

"The Breakaway" as the book's title, allowing me to appropriate it from the original profile of Rocky in *Chicago*. I would like to thank my family, most especially my life partner, Leah, for putting up with me throughout this journey, particularly on those many occasions where I had to beg off on obligations and trips in favor of late nights holed up at work in my home office.

Bryan Smith

Index

About the Author

BRYAN SMITH is a senior writer at *Chicago* magazine and a contributing editor for *Men's Health.* He is a two-time winner and six-time finalist for the National City and Regional Magazine Association's Writer of the Year award. His work has been featured in *The Best American Sports Writing*, *The Best American Newspaper Writing*, and the *Chicken Soup for the Soul* series.

Second to None: Chicago Stories celebrates the authenticity of a city brimming with rich narratives and untold histories. Spotlighting original, unique, and rarely explored stories, Second to None unveils a new and significant layer to Chicago's big-shouldered literary landscape.

Harvey Young, series editor